D1357653

Fifth Avenue

Avenue

The Best
Address

Fifth Avenue

The Best Address

Jerry E. Patterson

RIZZOLI
NEW YORK

Acknowledgments

The pleasantest words to write in a book are these in which I can express my gratitude
for the help I have received. At Rizzoli International Publications I am much indebted to my
editor David Morton, keen on the project from its first submission and generous with his
broad knowledge of New York City and its architecture. Also at Rizzoli I must thank Elizabeth White
and Ron Broadhurst, and at Worksight Emily Santoro and Scott Santoro. At the Museum
of the City of New York Eileen Kennedy and Elizabeth Ellis were most helpful
when I was seeking illustrations.

Susan Zeckendorf, my literary agent and friend, has borne delays with much appreciated
patience and unflagging enthusiasm for the book. I am grateful indeed to my friends
Anthony T. Mazzola and Michele Morgan Mazzola of Hearst Magazines for much practical advice
and assistance. Other supportive friends include Elizabeth Arnold, Peter Arnold, Brendan Cahill,
James F. Carr, Kathleen M. Doyle, Jacqueline Gomes, Julie Harman, Thomas F. Lecky,
Elizabeth Sims, Sheila Sullivan, and Frank Zachary.

And I must thank, as I have in previous books, the staff of the New York Society Library,
an institution well into its third century, that is one of the treasures of our city.

●

First published in the United States of America in 1998 by
RIZZOLI INTERNATIONAL PUBLICATIONS, INC.
300 Park Avenue South, New York, NY 10010

Copyright © 1998 Rizzoli International Publications, Inc.
All rights reserved.

No part of this publication may be reproduced in any
manner whatsoever without permission in writing from
Rizzoli International Publications, Inc.

Library of Congress Cataloging-in-Publication Data
Patterson, Jerry E.
    Fifth Avenue : the best address / Jerry E. Patterson
        p.   cm.
    Includes bibliographical references and index.
    ISBN 0-8478-2008-4
    1. Fifth Avenue (New York, N.Y.)—History. 2. Manhattan
(New York, N.Y.)—
    History. 3. New York (N.Y.)—History. I. Title.
F128.67.F4P38   1998   974-47410
                                                  CIP

Illustrations in this book are from the collection of the Museum
of the City of New York, except for those on pages 110, 111, and
187, which are from Avery Library at Columbia University, and
that on page 183, which is from the New-York Historical Society.

Design by Worksight

Printed in Singapore

Contents

●

1
From Village to Metropolis

Washington Square to Fourteenth Street

•

Old Henry Brevoort was the first man to live on Fifth Avenue. Nearly eighty years of age in 1824, when the avenue was laid out, he cultivated a farm straddling the crooked lane that would become Fifth Avenue. Between the Brevoort farm and the municipal cemetery below present-day Eighth Street lay a largely vacant twenty-one-acre estate owned by a charity called Sailors' Snug Harbor, which had received the land as a legacy from the estate of Robert Richard Randall when he died in 1801. He had endowed the charity for sailors "because," as he wrote in his will, "my father was a mariner; his fortune was made at sea." That was one way of putting it; actually, the elder Randall had been a successful pirate in the Caribbean. Through the entire low-lying area ran Minetta Water, a creek that was always ducking beneath the surface and which, even after the area had been drained and Fifth Avenue laid out, continued to flood basements. Much of the area was used as a dumping ground by the few inhabitants.

The Brevoort farm and the Randall estate were two or three miles north of New York City. Although New York was already nearly two hundred years old and had almost one hundred thousand citizens, these inhabitants and their numerous livestock—for there were no restrictions on keeping farm animals in town then or for many years afterward—occupied only the southern end of Manhattan Island, an area scarcely larger than it had been in Dutch days. Canal Street marked the northernmost limit of the city. Lack of cheap transportation kept most people within walking distance of their employment in the counting houses of Wall Street and Bowling Green or the docks and warehouses off Pearl Street. Farms like the Brevoorts' and wasteland lay north of the city, interspersed here and there with little settlements like the village of Greenwich, west of the Brevoort property.

The Brevoorts were Dutch who had once had a *van* before their name, and they had lived on the island of Manhattan since the 1630s, always farming the rocky and water-clogged soil of the island. Henry, the irascible patriarch of the family, known as the Old Gentleman to his long-suffering children, opposed any change and also any spending of money. He practiced Dutch industry and thrift: he sold vegetables from his truck garden on the corner of what became East Tenth Street and Fifth Avenue to markets downtown and imported rare birds for sale, caging them in a room in his house, where prospective customers came to admire their plumage and listen to their songs before buying. (His personal pet was a bear, which he kept chained in his front yard, where it was uneasily watched by his neighbors.) Like so many New Yorkers of colonial background, however, he drew the great wealth he eventually had from appreciation of his land. As William Armstrong wrote in 1846 in his book *The Aristocracy of New York,* Henry Brevoort, "by dint of persevering industry and rigid economy for a series of years, amassed considerable ready money, until the growth of the city eventually brought his small tract within its limits and by the corresponding rise of property literally turned it into money."

During Henry Brevoort's youth, New York City's prospects had not appeared golden. The years of the American Revolution had left the city battered and poor. Troops, British and American by turns, had roamed its streets; battles had been fought in its suburbs. Its citizens had bet on the wrong side: most of them were strongly Tory in sentiment and a quarter of them had left with the British troops when they finally evacuated the city in 1789. Nevertheless, against expectations, the city began to grow explosively in population and wealth in the early nineteenth century, mainly on account of its natural advantages as a port. It passed Philadelphia to become the most populous city in the new republic. In 1817 nearly one hundred thousand New Yorkers lived in seventeen thousand buildings. Some fine mansions lined lower Broadway, but most New Yorkers were miserably housed in cramped two- or three-story buildings densely packed along streets that horrified visitors with their mud and litter. No longer a neat Dutch village, New York was a booming, raucous, overcrowded city about to become a metropolis.

In 1807 the City Council finally noticed that Manhattan was spreading northward and decided that streets should be laid out and numbered in preparation for the day, apparently far distant, when the city limits would advance above Canal Street. Commissioners were appointed to survey the hills and dales above that busy street and to come up with a plan to ensure orderly settlement. The three commissioners and their surveyors worked for four years, laying out streets and avenues through orchards and gardens and combating diverse obstacles: an unusually long spell of bad weather, speculators who tried to buy up land ahead of them in the hope of securing advantageous sites, and hostility from the inhabitants.

Did the few New Yorkers living in this rather unattractive area welcome the surveyors as a sign that their city was maturing and that its future growth had to be planned efficiently to everyone's advantage? They did not. As they have throughout their history, New Yorkers viewed any changes proposed by the city government with suspicion and indignation. They set dogs on the surveying teams and pelted them with vegetables, as the commissioners reported in pained terms, and brought lawsuits against the city, beginning one of New York's longest-lasting traditions.

The commissioners decided on a gridiron plan for the new city, with "rectilinear and rectangular" streets. Their reasoning was that straight-sided and right-angled houses were the cheapest to build and the most convenient to live in, and also the easiest to locate and to describe in legal documents. The vague geography of the oldest part of the city, which had no street signs and few numbers, must have annoyed their orderly minds and determined them to make New York a city in which to find one's way without confusion. They ignored nature, preserving none of the natural contours of the land as they drained swamps, leveled hills, and cut down trees. "These men would have cut down the seven hills of Rome," a later authority asserted.

The Commissioners' Plan, as it was called, enabled the city to grow even more rapidly and to thrive as the center of American business. The 155 cross streets permitted citizens to get from the North (Hudson) River to the East River, and the twelve numbered avenues opened up the city northward. Aesthetic improvement was not the goal of the commissioners; better conditions for business were. John Randel, Jr., the principal surveyor, said bluntly that his plan helped in the "buying, selling, and improving of real estate." From the beginning there were complaints that little open space had been allotted: few squares were laid out, and no space was left for large parks. Complaints about the narrowness of the lots (they were only twenty-five feet wide) came from many sources. Narrow lots profoundly affected the look of the city for the next century, leading to streets lined with cramped houses that had little room for external variety. Baron de Trobriand, editor of the Parisian *Revue du Nouveau Monde*, wrote that the lots led to "the tiresome uniformity of the exteriors of houses and the tiresome sameness of the arrangements within—enabling the traveler, against his will, to know the inside of four-fifths of the houses in New York after he has put step into one."

To implement the Commissioners' Plan by laying out new streets and by grading and paving them, the city exercised the right of eminent domain to cut across private property in what the irritated citizenry considered a high-handed manner. Henry Brevoort was one of the most outraged property owners; he opposed the opening of the new Eleventh Street from Broadway to Fourth Avenue across his farm. Rich and well-connected— he was related to, among others, the Astors, already one of the richest families in the city—Brevoort was more successful than his neighbors. A contemporary account notes that "he resisted with such effect as to have that improvement abandoned." Eleventh Street never was cut through; it still halts for a short block between Broadway and Fourth Avenue. Grace

Episcopal Church was built on that site in 1846, on twelve city lots purchased from the Brevoort heirs for $58,600. Even then, Old Brevoort had the last word on the subject: the architect of Grace Church was James Renwick, Jr., who was his grandson.

Henry Brevoort, Jr., in 1827, told his friend Washington Irving, then living in Europe, that "the sole annoyance of the good old patriarch is the inroads of the corporation [the municipal government], who will persist in raising the value of his land by cutting it up into streets and burthening him by assessments. The Old Gentleman rebels and talks of the purity of the olden time but is obliged to submit."

Old Brevoort was one of the richest men in the city; when he died in 1841 at the age of ninety-four, his landed property was estimated to be worth over one million dollars, mainly for the eleven acres north of Washington Square, by that time the most desirable residential part of the city. The irony, of course, was that the changes he had opposed had immensely raised the value of his property.

The memorial tablet to Brevoort still in Grace Church notes that he was "in possession of the ground on which this church now stands, derived in unbroken descent from the first colonists of New Netherland.... His long life was free from guile and of spotless integrity."

On 22 March 1811 the commissioners issued a map that showed the future outline of the city as determined by their survey. The name *Fifth Avenue* appears for the first time on that map. The plan was greeted with skepticism; few believed that New York would ever grow sufficiently to need these guidelines. When the aged Marquis de Lafayette was visiting the city in 1824, he was shown the plan and found it too ambitious. He asked his hosts on the City Council, rather unkindly for a guest, "Do you expect Broadway and the Fifth Avenue will reach Albany?"

Fifth Avenue had a unique importance from the day the commissioners chose it to be the divider between the east and west sides of New York, the long chalk line down the island of Manhattan. Although no one conceived that Fifth Avenue would someday stretch six and a half miles up the island, it was clearly assumed that it would be the principal thoroughfare of upper New York City. It was wide and straight and eminently suitable for driving and promenading. Within a decade, well-to-do New Yorkers were building spacious houses on the avenue; within two decades fine churches were rising. Special qualities of fashion and class were attached to the name Fifth Avenue from the beginning. What is more remarkable is that they cling to the name more than a century and a half later.

The section of Fifth Avenue from the burying ground around Fifth Street to Thirteenth Street was "opened" that same year of 1824, which meant that lots were marked and the avenue and the side streets graded and paved. It was years before the proper paving material was found. Cobblestones were tried but were too uneven. Finally, so-called Belgian blocks, large flat stones fitted closely together, were laid down. Since all vehicles then had iron-rimmed wheels, the noise of traffic was thunderous. The streets of New York had already acquired an unattractive reputation, and not only for their noisiness. Snow was never hauled away; it just accumulated until melted by sun or rain. As William Rhinelander Stewart, resident and chronicler of the neighborhood, mildly remarked, "For most of the winter the streets were not inviting."

Fifth Avenue was planned on a gracious scale long before most European cities had cleaned up the medieval narrowness and crookedness of their streets—decades, for instance, before Baron Haussmann transformed Paris. Fifth Avenue was one hundred feet wide, encompassing a roadway of sixty feet and sidewalks on either side of twenty feet. Later the city permitted property owners to encroach fifteen feet on the sidewalks for stoops, yards, and porticoes. Residents took full advantage of this stipulation and, to the annoyance of city officials, added all sorts of ornamentations to the fronts of their houses. This created a fruitful source of argument that continued for the next eighty years until finally, in 1908, all encroachments were ordered removed by the powerful City Board of Estimate and the roadway was widened to accommodate the increasing automobile traffic.

The commissioners decided to mark the beginning of Fifth Avenue by laying out a square. The scrubby area they selected was the burying ground lying south of the new Eighth Street, where the unknown, indigent, and diseased had been buried since 1797, when the city bought ninety lots belonging to the farm of Elbert Herrin. A large potter's field (the name derives from a biblical reference to the purchase of a potter's field for use as a strangers' burial ground in Jerusalem) was a necessity in the late eighteenth and early nineteenth centuries, when New York had a large population of poor and was repeatedly swept by epidemics of yellow fever. Victims were buried wrapped in yellow shrouds so that those who had to handle the bodies would know they were being exposed to contagion. One of the reasons New Yorkers who could afford it continually moved north was to escape the "bad air" of the core city at the tip of the island. Bad air was a delicate name for the unhealthy miasma caused by defective sanitation, polluted water, and unburnt garbage.

Old accounts recorded that the bodies of the fever victims were dumped in wide but not very deep trenches, one on each side of the square, which were enclosed in fences and planted with trees. "It is computed," a guidebook of 1846 stated, "that over a hundred thousand bodies have been buried…in the nine acres of the square." The "hundred thousand" was sensationalism; recent scholarly enquiry into this subject estimates the number of bodies at about twenty-five thousand.

The field was also used for public executions, the bodies of the criminals being immediately buried in the area. Public executions were well attended, but they were certainly not for the squeamish. Peter Cooper, ironmonger and philanthropist, saw a man hanged there in 1810. "The recollection has chased me through life like a nightmare," Cooper wrote in his old age, "and whenever I look up I see him hanging, his head bent over on one side. There he remained for several hours, with the jeering crowd about him."

The dead were a presence for a long time in Washington Square. E. N. Tailer, a resident of the square most of his life, wrote, "I remember when heavy guns were drawn over the square, after it became a parade ground, that the weight broke through the ground into the trenches in which the dead were buried and crushed the tops of some of the coffins." Even more gruesomely, when sidewalks were opened, glimpses were caught of yellow sheets.

There were no more burials after 1826, when the ground was leveled and filled in. The space became a drilling ground for numerous groups of volunteers who belonged to civic regiments and was first known as the Washington Parade Ground. Shortly after, it became Washington Square and was officially opened to the public on the Fourth of July 1828. Trees were planted and walks laid out. The neighborhood was supplied with water from a well in the park. The fact that the well stood in the middle of a cemetery did not seem to discourage its use, and the water was esteemed for its clarity and softness.

The streets surrounding the square were then ready for the construction of private houses. The neighborhood, far but not inconveniently so from noisy and crowded "downtown," was regarded from its opening as one of the best in New York. Around 1830, prominent citizens lived around the

Some of the finest Greek revival houses in the United States line the north side of Washington Square. This photograph, showing 21 to 25 Washington Square North, was taken by Berenice Abbott in the 1930s. At the time, the houses were already a century old, and their continued survival is a remarkable exception to New York's constant reinvention of itself.

Battery, on Broadway further uptown, around St. Paul's churchyard, and on the streets leading off Broadway, such as Bond and Bleecker. But those streets were already becoming crowded and lined with commercial establishments. Earlier New Yorkers, even the most successful, had not been ashamed to live next door to the warehouses and offices where they earned their livelihood, or even "above the shop," but around 1830 a great change took place in the thinking and ambitions of the well-to-do: Suddenly, it became unfashionable to live between shops and warehouses and saloons—of which New York had more than its share—enduring noise from the streets, and there was a marked migration "uptown." By 1837, of 140 pews at Grace Church, then at Broadway and Rector Street, at least 95 belonged to people who had moved above Canal Street. Lafayette Place opened in 1827, and La Grange Terrace, named for Lafayette's home in France, soon after. Both of these were a few blocks east of Fifth Avenue and immediately became fashionable addresses.

The famous row of austerely elegant houses in the Greek revival style, still in part standing on the north side of Washington Square, dates from the 1830s and was the first built in the new neighborhood of Lower Fifth Avenue. The residents were mostly rich merchants like Saul Alley, James Boorman, John Johnston, William C. Rhinelander, and Thomas Suffern. The term *merchant* was then miscellaneously used: most so-called merchants were importer-exporters and small-scale manufacturers rather than shopkeepers, although many had begun by keeping a shop. The first householders in Washington Square dealt in whale oil, iron, tobacco, and sugar. Among the merchants were scattered a few bankers, attorneys, and physicians.

The land on which their new houses stood was not freehold; it was held on long leases from the Sailors' Snug Harbor. The lots were either twenty-seven or thirty-two feet wide; the narrower houses rented for $130 a year, the wider ones for $150. They were uniformly three stories tall with a basement entry and dormer windows on the fourth-floor attics. The main floors were raised considerably above street level, creating the characteristic New York stoop; the steps leading up to the front door usually had delicate iron banisters. The lots on which they stood were ninety feet deep, and the spaces behind the houses extending to Eighth Street were gardens with flowerbeds and trellises. These trellises figure in many books of reminiscence of the time, which usually dwell on their flowery and attractive appearance. Delicacy prevented the authors from saying that they masked the path to the outdoor privies, which even such first-class dwellings still depended on, and provided protection for necessary trips in bad weather.

The houses had addresses on Washington Square. The continuation of the street to the west of the square was named Waverly Place, on petition of the residents, to honor Sir Walter Scott. Fifth Street leading out of the square was named Washington Place between Broadway and the square. The setting was urban but uncrowded. The planting in the square, the trees on Fifth Avenue, and the gardens behind the houses gave the neighborhood an almost pastoral air.

One of the first families on Washington Square was the Rhinelanders: William Rhinelander built at number 14, the first house on the northwest corner of the new Fifth Avenue and the square. The Rhinelander family settled in New York in the seventeenth century. At first they imported china and glass, a major business in the colonial era because America produced so little of each; then they ran a bakery and, finally, became successful sugar merchants. However, the foundation of the great Rhinelander fortune was land; the family owned blocks of farmland in what became the Upper East Side of Manhattan. The new Rhinelander house on Washington Square was designed by Richard Upjohn, also the architect of Trinity Church on Wall Street and of the Church of the Ascension on Fifth Avenue, built at about the same time. There was something vaguely ecclesiastical about the Rhinelander house, too: it had a granite entrance and an impressive forty-two-foot frontage facing the square. William Rhinelander's daughter Serena lived in the house until her death in 1914; it was torn down in 1953 after highly vocal but useless protest from preservationists. Her nephew, William Rhinelander Stewart, lived at 7 Washington Square, and other members of the family built in the new neighborhood.

With an open square in front and elegant neighbors, the area attracted more well-to-do New Yorkers; building began northward from Washington Square on Fifth Avenue. James Lenox, whose father was one of the great property owners in the city, lived at number 53 on the northeast corner of Twelfth Street. Robert Bowne Minturn, head of a large firm of merchants originally dealing in whale oil, built across Fifth Avenue at number 60 on the northwest corner.

Life was pleasant on Lower Fifth Avenue. Many of the inhabitants, like the Rhinelanders, were related to each other; they could easily drop in on relatives, and at a time when entertaining was centered on homes and upper-class women did not venture far from their own hearths, social life was encompassed within a few blocks. Although rich, they lived in comfort rather than luxury and in what they fancied was old-time simplicity. It was fashionable to be "careful with money." Until after the Civil War, ostentation was unwelcome.

The hours for meals among well-to-do New Yorkers were quite different from today's. It was not a particularly early-rising era, at least for the business classes. Men breakfasted at around nine o'clock before they went "downtown" to their offices. It was important that the wife or mother be present and "pour the tea" (or coffee) and "make the toast" for the man before he set out; these two gestures at breakfast were of great symbolic significance in family life, although they could have easily been performed by the numerous servants these households kept. There was no lunch. Dinner was not later than two o'clock, the men coming uptown for it and returning afterward to work. When they quit work for the day and returned home at eight o'clock or thereabout, tea was served. This meal was not to be confused with afternoon tea, which became a custom only in the late 1870s. Tea before the Civil War was a substantial meal, supper, in fact. But supper then was usually a late-night meal, and at dances the refreshments, served around midnight, were called supper.

A notable domestic change as the nineteenth century progressed was in the hours for meals: the dinner hour moved steadily forward, first to four or five o'clock, then to six or seven o'clock; lunch began to be eaten by businessmen near their offices in company with other men; and women ate a midday meal at home or as guests in other homes; tea became an afternoon snack served at four or five o'clock, and supper vanished altogether except as party refreshments.

The many front yards on Fifth Avenue gave it a small-town appearance. Flowers were planted, especially geraniums, which were hardy and made a brave show. Even then it took tough plants to survive in New York air. These little gardens were no longer possible when the avenue was widened. During the warm months window awnings were ubiquitous, as the narrow brownstone houses could be suffocating; in Washington Square they were of uniform green-and-white stripes.

The rich businessmen who lived on Lower Fifth Avenue did not go to their downtown offices every day; they transacted a good deal of business at home, a holdover from the time when they had lived above the shop. When callers came on business, they were generally received by the man of the house in the dining room or library if he had no office at home; the drawing room was regarded as the preserve of the mistress of the household, to whom casual callers on business did not merit an introduction. Countless novels of the time tell of a bright young clerk who goes to his boss's house with papers for him to sign and catches a glimpse of a daughter with consequences that end in his becoming the son-in-law and heir to the business. John D. Crimmins, whose father was a contractor, remembered going to some of these houses in his youth. The businessmen "had no hesitation," he recalled, "in receiving in their homes after business hours the people whom they employed. I remember distinctly before gas was generally introduced, how very economical in its use those who had it were. In the absence of the butler the gentleman of the house would often walk to the door with his visitor and then lower the gas."

The father of the family often stood, in those early days, at the gate of the little yards that the city permitted, to take the air, inspect the flowers, and greet the neighbors. Such simple manners disappeared as the businessmen grew richer, downtown offices larger and more sophisticated, travel to them easier, and Fifth Avenue more fashionable. After about 1870 one no longer saw gentlemen at their gates. Women never went to offices. Even the kindly Abram S. Hewitt, who lived on Washington Square and was the mayor of New York in 1886, once told the daughter of a friend, who was collecting for a benevolent cause, "You must call on me uptown [i.e., at home]; a lady should not enter a man's office, even for charity."

The main building of the University of the City of New York, called New York University after 1896, stood on the east side of Washington Square and was more than adequate in accommodating the university's student body: some of its rooms were rented out as apartments to artists and writers. The building was demolished in 1894, when the undergraduate division of the university moved to the Bronx. Undergraduates returned to Washington Square in 1973.

A neighborhood girl, Catherine Elizabeth Havens, born in 1839, kept a diary when she was ten years old. Her family lived "in 9th Street" between University Place and Fifth Avenue. (Then, and for long after, New Yorkers lived *in* rather than *on* a street.) "It is a beautiful house," she wrote, "and has glass sliding doors with birds of Paradise sitting on palm trees painted on them. And back of our dining room is a piazza and a grape vine and we have lots of Isabella grapes every fall. It has a parlor in front and the library in the middle and the dining room at the back." She obviously did not go far from home. "Fifth Avenue is very muddy above 18th Street," she wrote disdainfully, "and there are no blocks of houses as there are down town, but only two or three on a block."

When the merchant gentry moved uptown, their institutions, especially schools and churches, soon followed. At 1 Fifth Avenue was a seminary for young ladies run by the Misses Lucy and Mary Green, who came from an established New York family. Their faculty of young men teachers included at various times Elihu Root, later U.S. secretary of state and winner of the Nobel Peace Prize; John Bigelow, later minister to France; and John Fiske, who became America's chief exponent of Darwin's new theory of evolution. Winston Churchill's mother, Jennie Jerome, was a student there at one time.

Higher education arrived in the neighborhood in 1831, when New York University, first called the University of the City of New York and strongly Presbyterian, opened on the east side of Washington Square. While the school was being built, convicts from the state prison at Sing Sing, in Westchester County, were employed in cutting stone. That displeased the professional stonemasons of the city, who rioted in 1834 in the square and had to be dispersed by the militia, which patrolled the park for days. Architecturally, the original building was Gothic, undoubtedly meant to remind people of old and important British educational institutions in the same style. Despite the elegant style of its building and the prominence of many of its teachers, the new institution had trouble attracting students and was obliged to rent out apartments in its building, mostly to artists and architects. Even the chapel was subdivided into rooms for rent. The building, which had become very dilapidated, was torn down in 1894.

The university had the solid and very practical support of the residents of Washington Square and Lower Fifth Avenue; most of the donors of large sums were residents of the square; in 1853, when there was a sizable deficit, they were the principal contributors. Sons of the early residents of the square attended the new school. John Taylor Johnston, for example, whose father had been one of the first residents, graduated from New York University. He later became a railroad executive at the Central Railroad of New Jersey and founding president of the Metropolitan Museum of Art. Like many others of the second generation, he stayed in the neighborhood; in 1856 he built his own house, the first marble mansion in New York, at number 8, on the southwest corner of Eighth Street and Fifth Avenue. He avidly collected paintings by contemporary French and German artists and also by American painters. He owned paintings by Winslow Homer, Thomas Cole, and Frederic Edwin Church. Crowded by his art treasures, in 1860 he converted the stable behind his house into a gallery. Hard hit by the economic depression that began in 1873, he sold his collection of paintings at auction in 1876, two hundred oils bringing three hundred thousand dollars, a large sum at the time. In the 1880s his finances recovered, and he had his house redecorated by Louis Comfort Tiffany in the most up-to-date style, which included latticework, panels of East Indian teakwood and colored glass tiles around the fireplace, and a profusion of Middle Eastern and Chinese ceramics.

Churches were bound to be found near schools. Educational and religious institutions were inextricably linked in those days; most schools were part of, or sponsored by, churches. In New York's history no institutions have moved more often than its churches. A pattern was established early on: as neighborhoods changed from residential to commercial, congregations shrank and real-estate values increased; churches took their profits by selling up and following their members. Although it was an age devoted to the outward manifestations of Christianity, congregations seem to have been quite unsentimental about their church buildings.

The first churches to open on Fifth Avenue were Presbyterian and Episcopalian. That was not surprising: the neighborhood was rich and those two Protestant denominations, along with the ancient Dutch Reformed church, had long included most well-to-do New Yorkers. Of the 150 churches in the city in 1837, the Presbyterians, with 39, had more than any other denomination; the Episcopalians had 29. By 1846 there were 215 churches in the city, a phenomenal growth in little more than a decade; 41 were Episcopalian, 32 Presbyterian. The figures reflect the constant merging of congregations, the closing of some churches, and the building of new. While not often changing denominations, parishioners followed popular preachers from one congregation to another.

Many of the new families in Washington Square and Lower Fifth Avenue were of Scottish descent and Presbyterian in religion. The First Presbyterian Church, formerly on Wall Street, rose on the west side of the avenue between Eleventh and Twelfth streets and opened for services in 1846; its sanctuary seated between twelve hundred and fifteen hundred people. The edifice was estimated to have cost seventy-five

One of the first churches to be built in the vicinity of Washington Square was the First Presbyterian Church on the west side of Fifth Avenue between Eleventh and Twelfth streets. Designed by Joseph C. Wells and completed in 1846, the Gothic Revival church served the many merchants and professionals of Scottish descent who settled around Washington Square and Lower Fifth Avenue in the 1830s.

thousand dollars. For the Episcopalians in the neighborhood, the Episcopal Church of the Ascension at Tenth Street was built in 1841, designed by Richard Upjohn. In 1888–89 the church was extensively re-decorated. The finest American artists of the time did some of their best work there: Stanford White, the architect, designed a new chancel; Augustus Saint-Gaudens, the sculptor, adorned it with angelic figures; and Maitland Armstrong, a stained-glass artist who lived on Tenth Street, provided mosaics. The most important work was the magnificent painting of the Ascension by John La Farge, which was paid for by the Misses Rhinelander of Washington Square, generous benefactors of the Episcopal church in New York. In Washington Square there was a Dutch Reformed Church, erected in 1840, formerly known as the South

Reformed Dutch Church, which was ancient, having been established in the time of Peter Stuyvesant. All of these churches charged rent for their pews and naturally attracted the well-to-do.

It was a churchgoing age, at least among the upper middle class and the rich in New York City, although church attendance among the general population was not high. The concern that the well-to-do and devout felt for their benighted fellow citizens was reflected in the large number of "mission" churches supported by wealthier congregations and scattered among poorer neighborhoods in the city. The "mission," of course, was conversion.

City authorities strongly backed the spirit of the times. Mayoral regulations of 1817 laid down a strict observance of Sunday: no work, no buying or selling except of fish and milk (because of the danger of those comestibles spoiling rapidly), no hunting, no sport, and, inexplicably, "no wading horses in the river." The regulations allowed churches to put chains across streets during services in order to prevent the passing of noisy carriages and stagecoaches. Churches were still built along parish lines as neighborhood institutions. They needed to be near their congregants' homes because families usually walked to church, it being considered improper to drive even if one had a private carriage. Walking to church was a good way for young men and women to see each other at a time when "dating" was not permitted and, in fact, unknown among respectable families. When a young man was seen often walking to church with a young woman and her family, it was assumed that he was an admitted suitor for her hand.

Although New York was never a Puritan town, these churches were evangelical and the services were "low," with very little ritual. Trinity and other Episcopal churches did not have "vested" choirs; choristers wore their everyday clothes. Trinity first had a vested choir on the occasion of the Prince of Wales's attendance during his visit to the city in 1860, when the service was made as Anglican as possible in compliment to the future king. The innovation did not pass without comment from the more convinced evangelicals. Grace Church did not have choir robes until more than thirty years later.

For work, of course, there had to be transportation to the city from Washington Square and Lower Fifth Avenue, which were regarded as distant. Businessmen often walked to their offices, but women of position rarely walked anywhere except to church, certainly never unaccompanied. Very few people, even among the well-to-do, kept carriages, which were a major expense, entailing not only the purchase of horses and a vehicle and the hiring of a coachman but also building or renting a stable, usually located at some distance from the residence to avoid smells and noise. Transportation was generally by stagecoach. Each stage company ran about thirty vehicles. In 1844 there were 220 liveried stages in the city "running like comets in every direction." Lined up, observers concluded with the American passion for such calculations, they would reach nearly two miles. Stages held six people on either side, but when crinolines—skirts worn over a sort of iron cage that extended the skirt to enormous circular dimensions—became popular about mid-century, women's skirts took up so much room, men complained, that only three people could sit on each side. If you were a man you could ride on the outside, climbing up by iron footholds. The driver attached a leather strap to his leg that connected with the rear door and by which the door could be opened or closed. A box beneath the driver's seat held the nickel fares. He kept an eye on that box, and if a fare was not deposited, the offender was vocally singled out and shamed.

The first "omnibuses," or horsecars, appeared in 1830. By mid-century there were horsecar lines ("buses") on Second, Third, Sixth, and Eighth avenues, and eventually on Fifth. Horsecar lines ran on rails, the vehicles drawn by horses or mules. Each car held about fourteen passengers. On the single-horse lines, you handed your fare to the driver through a hole in the top of the bus and in due time received change in a little green, pink, or blue envelope according to the amount of change coming to you. Hamilton Fish Armstrong, who rode the stages from his home on West Tenth Street just off Fifth Avenue to the Allan-Stevenson School uptown about mid-century, remembered: "Often there was much bowing by gentlemen offering to pass along the money for ladies, and sometimes an argument, in which everyone joined, as to whether or not a certain fare had been paid."

During the Civil War, when specie payment was suspended, there was no small change and fares were paid in postage stamps, which in hot weather stuck to everything. You pulled a string attached to the driver's leg when you wanted to be set down. The floors were covered with straw in bad weather to absorb mud and snow; the cars were notoriously smelly and uncomfortable. Later, "long" horsecars were introduced; drawn by two horses, these had front and rear platforms with both a driver and a conductor. Fifth Avenue, in keeping with its image, received the best. One commentator described the service: "Gaudily painted buses, drawn by a team of horses, plied a route from Washington Square North. These omnibuses were the handsomest in the city. They were drawn by four horses and had the names of distinguished Americans—Thomas Jefferson, Benjamin Franklin, De Witt Clinton—emblazoned on their sides, sometimes accompanied by painted portraits."

Fifth Avenue was suited to fashionable traffic. Mabel Osgood Wright remembered from her childhood, about mid-century,

> …nowhere in America were so many fine horses to be seen. Men and women on horseback coming from the side streets on their way to the bridle path, open landaus with beautifully gowned women, more formal coaches with high springs and double folding steps to bridge the greatest distance…. Elderly people usually rode in these and the smart young men and women…were frequently seen driving the two-wheeled dogcarts, sometimes with a single horse, sometimes tandem. Indeed Fifth Avenue was akin to a horse show….

In 1825 the first gas pipes for the city south of Fourteenth Street were laid by the New York Gas Company, and gas lamps began to illuminate the avenues with soft, yellowish light. By 1847 they extended up Fifth Avenue as far as Eighteenth Street. The lamplighters, invariably tall men who had a reputation for self-importance and were ponderous about their work, turned them on each twilight with a valve at the end of a long wand; high winds frequently blew out the gas. There were a few private streetlights, and a tradition that the mayor of New York had a pair of lights at his gate, a mark of honor that he got to keep even after his term of office had expired.

After the Civil War, telegraph poles appeared on Fifth Avenue connecting the upper and lower parts of the city and immensely facilitating business. Telegraphy could be regarded as a neighborhood industry since Samuel F. B. Morse had invented the telegraph while he was teaching at New York University. New Yorkers, whose city was already the American capital of communications, seized on the new invention, and city streets were soon a forest of useful though far from attractive poles. The rich had buzzer systems installed in their houses so that a telegraph boy could be quickly summoned from headquarters to pick up messages. This invention, and a little later the telephone, brought the business city, once miles away, closer to Lower Fifth Avenue. The area began to lose its bucolic atmosphere.

When the novelist Mrs. Burton Harrison (Constance Cary), a Virginian who had lived in Paris, came to settle in New York after the Civil War, she wrote, "Fifth Avenue, fringed on either side with telegraph poles, was abominably paved with irregular blocks of stone, so that a drive to the [Central] Park and 'away uptown to 50th Street' was accompanied by much wear and tear to the physical and nervous system."

Lower Fifth Avenue quickly became the center of fashionable life in New York. The young Henry Brevoorts, son and daughter-in-law of the difficult Old Gentleman, built the finest house, on the northwest corner of Fifth Avenue and Ninth Street on land the old man had farmed. Put up in 1834 and perhaps designed (no positive evidence exists) by Ithiel Town and Alexander Jackson Davis, masters of the Greek Revival style, it was freestanding with a garden entrance on one side, a curved window on the other, and Ionic columns ornamenting either side of the door. Hamilton Fish Armstrong remembered that "it was painted mouse color; inside the spacious rooms and halls were mostly a greenish cafe-au-lait or chocolate." It had a large yard in front blooming with lilac, rose of Sharon, and forsythia surrounded by a handsome iron fence. The house was luxurious in every respect. The first floor contained a drawing room flanked by large parlors, creating an enfilade for entertaining, and a dining room with

This early photograph shows the Henry Brevoort, Jr., house as it was in the 1850s. The Brevoort name has been prominent on Lower Fifth Avenue for two centuries, and the history of elegant entertaining on the avenue begins with the Brevoort house. Brevoort and his southern wife, Laura Carson Brevoort, building on the fortune left by Brevoort's famously tightfisted father, received guests on an exceptionally grand scale by conservative New York standards. The house was demolished in 1925.

pantry (the kitchen was in the basement). The second floor contained five bedrooms and boasted a bathroom with a tub that used a faucet and drain, the very latest in sanitary equipment. In the rear, opening on West Ninth Street, was a stable with a large loft for hay and straw, "excellent for roughhousing and games," Armstrong remembered. The fact that children could play in a barn on Fifth Avenue as late as 1903 shows how rural some aspects of New York life were at the end of the nineteenth century.

In 1850, the Brevoort house was sold to the de Rham family, also old New Yorkers, who lived in it until 1921; it was demolished in 1925, and replaced by the fifteen-story Fifth Avenue Hotel, still standing. On nearby West Eleventh Street the younger Brevoort built four other houses as wedding gifts for his children. Still existing, they, like the houses on the north side of Washington Square, have had a long life, not without vicissitudes. In March 1970 one was being used by a terrorist group, the Weathermen, as a bomb factory, when it blew up; fortunately only one person, a Weatherman, was killed.

At number 17 lived Henry Bergh. A notable defender of animals, he was the founder, in 1866, of the Society for the Prevention of Cruelty to Animals. This was the first humane society in the United States, antedating—a strange commentary—the Society for the Prevention of Cruelty to Children, founded by another Fifth Avenue resident, Elbridge T. Gerry, in 1874. Bergh was originally outraged by the treatment of horses on New York's streets, especially the overworked beasts that pulled the omnibuses and stages. He was constantly on the alert for mistreatment and reported abusive drivers to their management. Needless to say, he was not popular with the drivers, who loudly sang satirical songs about the man they considered a busybody.

At number 53 on the northeast corner of Twelfth Street lived James Lenox, a chilly and unapproachable bachelor who was heir to one of New York's great real-estate fortunes, based on the family farm, thirty acres that lay on a slight rise between East Sixty-fourth and Seventieth streets still called Lenox Hill. He was a Scottish Presbyterian of the strictest observance. His biographer wrote of him, "He staked out his long course, hoed his own row, [and] paddled his own canoe…." James Lenox was one of the greatest book collectors of all time: he owned a Gutenberg Bible, the first to come to America (he paid a stupendous three thousand dollars for it), and the manuscript of Washington's Farewell Address, among other treasures. His collection ranked with the greatest European libraries. New York had no public libraries at the time, and Lenox allowed scholars to use his books on a rather limited basis: he stood over them nervously while they took notes. He confined his bookbinder to a vestibule where the worker could not even glimpse the treasures of the library. Lenox also owned paintings, including the first work by J. M. W. Turner to reach this country. In 1870, Lenox, who had always refused to exhibit his books, suddenly gave the entire collection to a trust and had a building erected for it on Fifth Avenue between Seventieth and Seventy-first streets by Richard Morris Hunt. Two decades later it became one of the foundations of the New York Public Library. The Lenox family home at 53 Fifth Avenue became Presbyterian House, with offices for missions, women's groups, and church construction. Encompassing the houses of Lenox, John Taylor Johnston, and farther up the avenue, August Belmont and others, this neighborhood contained more art treasures than any city of nineteenth-century America.

These large and important houses were usually detached from their neighbors by yards and gardens, since the neighborhood was still only partly settled. In 1851 between numbers 1 and 136 Fifth Avenue (Washington Square to Twenty-third Street) there were still thirty-two vacant lots and fifteen other lots were described as "now building."

The public amenities of the neighborhood were expanded when the Brevoort Hotel, the first hotel on Fifth Avenue, opened in 1854, formed by joining three already existing buildings, Brevoort family property, on the northeast corner of Eighth Street. The hotel was only five stories high; as yet there were no elevators. The Brevoort, in keeping with the neighborhood, was considered New York's most dignified hotel, much favored by visiting Europeans.

A few years later, in 1861, New York's premier restaurant, Delmonico's, opened in a house that had formerly belonged to the shipowner Moses Hicks Grinnell on the northeast corner of Fourteenth Street and Fifth Avenue. The Delmonico family—two brothers from Switzerland and their four nephews—had first opened a restaurant about 1827 on William Street. The restaurant had already moved no fewer than seven times and, before it finally closed in 1925, would move twice more, always northward on Fifth Avenue as its clientele moved uptown.

New York society was gradually making Fifth Avenue the "social spine of New York," as journalists loved to call it. It was popular for promenading, a sure sign of its status as a boulevard resembling the great boulevards in Europe. Promenading was primarily a male sport. To promenade, one dressed oneself in one's best clothes. In late nineteenth-century New York that meant wearing London-made fashions and comporting oneself in what was presumed to be an English manner. Mrs. Burton Harrison, the novelist, remembered, that crop of golden youths who may be seen any afternoon in the Fifth Avenue, with trousers turned up [i.e., with cuffs, then unusual; when small boys saw these "dudes" wearing trousers with cuffs they yelled, "Must be rainin' today in London!"], well-fitted body coats with large *boutonnière* of white flowers, and high hats, striding along as if sprinting for a prize, and swinging their sticks with diligence—enough like the original article to be scarcely distinguishable from it at close approach.

The Brevoort Hotel opened in 1854 at the northeast corner of Fifth Avenue and Eighth Street. With the advent of the literary and artistic communities in Greenwich Village, the Brevoort welcomed the better-heeled creative figures of the early twentieth century. The hotel was modernized in 1946, only to be demolished in 1953. On the same block at 21 Fifth Avenue (far left), James Renwick, who married a Brevoort, built a house in 1840 that was occupied by Mark Twain between 1904 and 1908.

The Delmonico family opened their first restaurant in New York in 1828. By 1861 they were able to buy the house of Moses Grinnell, a prominent shipowner. The Delmonicos spent a year converting the house on the northeast corner of Fifth Avenue and Fourteenth Street into the city's best-known restaurant serving French fare. The menu listed no fewer than three hundred dishes, the sophistication of which ranged from plain rice pudding to coquille de faisan.

For the ladies the time-consuming paying of weekly calls on one's relatives and friends was an indispensable part of upper-class life. Ladies "took a day" (Mrs. Astor, Mondays; Mrs. Brevoort, Tuesdays) for receiving visitors; as the city became unmanageably large and the traffic impeding, days were consolidated in certain neighborhoods, which meant that the energetic could get through a remarkable number of calls in a few hours. In Washington Square, the day was Friday. Tea as a meal became popular in the 1870s, and on their days, hostesses served tea or hot chocolate or bouillon, little cakes bought from Dean's, the fashionable baker, and watercress sandwiches. These were winter events; ladies of this class spent their summers out of town.

The specialness of Fifth Avenue was well established in popular culture: as early as 1868 there was already a song by William H. Lingard named for the street, followed two years later by dance music, "The Fifth Avenue Galop" (the galop was a fast dance like the polka). Edward Harrigan, of the acting team of Harrigan and Hart, wrote "South Fifth Avenue" in 1881, satirizing the snobbishness of the avenue. There were plays, too: in 1877, at Booth's Theatre, *Fifth Avenue*, an unmemorable comedy about pushy Fifth Avenue parents, an heiress daughter, and a chinless British aristocrat she did not want to marry, ran for a month.

A few blocks east and west of the rich and dignified district around Washington Square, where tea and watercress sandwiches were being consumed, were, however, very different neighborhoods. To the west was Greenwich Village, still literally a village, long settled and regarded as both bucolic and salubrious. When New York was attacked by one of its frequent epidemics of yellow or another deadly fever, New Yorkers who could afford it emigrated for the hot months, when the fevers generally occurred, to Greenwich Village, where they rented little houses or sometimes pitched tents on vacant lots to take advantage of the open air. They stayed until the first frost, which was thought to clear the atmosphere. Later, Sixth Avenue became a shopping district; householders on Lower Fifth Avenue sent their servants over to Sixth Avenue, where between West Third and West Tenth streets there were shops on both sides of the avenue that supplied most needs.

To the east of Fifth Avenue was a deplorable district that included stables for the houses on Washington Square and Lower Fifth Avenue. There were a lot of taverns along Broadway and an astonishing number of brothels. Mercer Street, just three blocks from Washington Square, was the main promenade of streetwalkers; respectable women ventured there at their peril. For years there was agitation to "clean up" this district but with few results.

The glory days of Lower Fifth Avenue were the decades between the 1830s and 1880s. In the political divisions of the city it was known as the "American ward"; even in 1875 only a third of its population was foreign-born, a low percentage in the Manhattan of the time. By the 1870s, evening receptions, formerly the principal way of entertaining one's friends, were on the decline. Afternoon tea, served around four or five o'clock, became popular. One of the advantages for women was that bonnets and street dress could be worn; it was not necessary to change into elaborate evening dress. The only men in attendance were old beaux who had nothing to do and some professional men who made their own hours. Depending upon her capacity for tea and small sandwiches, a diligent lady could accomplish many calls in one afternoon, thus catching up on her social obligations in a single day.

By the 1890s Lower Fifth Avenue was regarded as the quaint relic of a simpler age. The old families around Washington Square held on, but they were thought of as "cave dwellers," out-of-date though enviably patrician and rich. In 1891 the area below Fourteenth Street was described by the press as "a picturesque oasis where the aristocratic air of old Knickerbocker stateliness lingers amid a commonplace environment. The six blocks between Washington Square and Thirteenth Street are a unique corner of New York."

A French art dealer, René Gimpel, who had a shop on Upper Fifth Avenue and spent part of each year in New York, said of Washington Square in 1919: "One could almost believe oneself in London in this square, with its two-story brick houses so regular and alike. The square, placed halfway between the lower part of the city, that gigantic hive of business, and the residential district with its thousands of cars, seems as if by magic to belong to another town, another town really situated hundreds of leagues off…."

Albert Ullmann wrote elegiacally in 1917 of Lower Fifth Avenue, "…this portion of New York appears to many persons the most delectable. It has a kind of established repose which is not of frequent occurrence in other quarters of the long, shrill city; it has a riper, richer, more honorable look than any of the upper ramifications of the great longitudinal thorough-fare—the look of having had something of a social history."

Many of these residents were still quite involved in the civic affairs of New York. William Rhinelander Stewart, whose family had lived on Washington Square since it was laid out, was the projector of the arch erected in the square, which became one of New York's most beloved landmarks. On the last day of April 1889 the city had elaborately and enthusiastically celebrated the centennial of the inauguration of George Washington as President of the United States, one of the major events of the American Revolution taking place in New York City. A temporary triumphal arch in the Roman style ingeniously made of wood painted to simulate marble was designed by the architect Stanford White to commemorate the event. It stood between the first two houses on Fifth Avenue, about one hundred feet north of the square.

New Yorkers were dazzled by the majestic white edifice, which gave Fifth Avenue a worthy entrance, and there was a demand for a permanent arch in marble. Stanford White was again the architect. Excavations for the arch uncovered numerous coffins from the time when the square was a potter's field; they were decently reinterred. The marble arch was completed in May 1892, a year in which New York civic pride, usually in short supply, exploded: the glorious four hundredth anniversary of the discovery of America saw the move of Columbia University to Morningside Heights ("the Acropolis of America"), the laying of the cornerstone of the Cathedral of St. John the Divine, and the unveiling of the statue of Christopher Columbus at the southwest corner of Central Park.

Lower Fifth Avenue was still low-rise. Tall apartment buildings were not erected for another two decades, as it was thought the light soil south of Fourteenth Street would not sustain their weight. However, the population was changing as the neighborhood was increasingly penetrated by immigrants, especially Italians. Just as puzzling to the "cave dwellers" were the "Bohemians" who invaded in large numbers after 1900. Bohemians were not really feckless squatters, as the name might imply, but people in the arts, or trying to be in the arts, and their patrons, many of whom were distinctly upper-class (the heiresses Mabel Dodge and

For years the anniversary of Washington's inauguration on 30 April 1789 was elaborately celebrated, but never more so than on its centennial in 1889, when this great temporary arch (made of wood treated to look like marble) spanned Fifth Avenue on its first block. Most of the trees pictured were lost when the avenue was widened a few years later.

Gertrude Vanderbilt Whitney, for example). Although drunken parties were certainly not unknown, and in recollection became legendary, gathering for tea in an artist's studio was much more characteristic of the *vie de Bohème* in New York.

The Bohemians made Lower Fifth Avenue part of Greenwich Village, which rapidly expanded eastward, crossing Sixth Avenue and gradually including the entire area between the Hudson River and Broadway. Old

In 1909, New Yorkers again celebrated with great pomp, this time to mark the tercentenary of Henry Hudson's discovery on 2 September 1609 of New York Bay and the river that bears his name. Bridges and prominent buildings were outlined in light bulbs on an unprecedented scale, as seen in this photograph of the Washington Arch in Washington Square, designed by Stanford White in 1892 to replace the temporary arch.

residents of Lower Fifth Avenue thought of Greenwich Village, when they thought of it at all, as a distant neighborhood where the servants lived and did the shopping. Greenwich Village was never more than middle class, while from the beginning, Lower Fifth Avenue was distinctly upper class. The surviving nineteenth-century houses in both neighborhoods plainly show this. The residents of Lower Fifth Avenue certainly never thought of themselves as living in Greenwich Village. After the early years of the

twentieth century, however, they found that other New Yorkers and gawk-
ers from out of town thought an address on Lower Fifth Avenue was in
the "Village," with all that implied in the way of liberty and frivolity.

The conservative old Brevoort Hotel began a new role as a center of
Bohemia: Edna St. Vincent Millay, Isadora Duncan, Eugene O'Neill, and
John Dos Passos were constantly to be found in its famous basement cafe.
Actors at the Provincetown Theatre on MacDougal Street used to save
up for a month to have one good meal at the Brevoort. Theodore Dreiser,
who lived in many addresses in the Village and was involved with any
number of women, sometimes concurrently, used to take the reigning
favorite to lunch at the Brevoort, where he was in terror of being seen by
other girl friends passing by the large windows facing on Fifth Avenue.
Nathanael West, author of *Miss Lonelyhearts*, lived there from 1935 to
1936, as did James T. Farrell while he was writing *The Young Manhood of
Studs Lonigan*.

John Dos Passos, who lived in 1922 in Washington Mews on Fifth Avenue
between Washington Square and East Eighth Street, often visited the
hotel. In *The 42d Parallel,* the first volume of his great trilogy, *U.S.A.,* he
depicts the way the hotel looked to newcomers. Eleanor Stoddard arrives
with a girl friend for the first time in New York City, where they have only
one friend, Freddy. "Freddy met them at the train and took them to get
rooms at the Brevoort. He said it was a little far from the theatre but much
more interesting than an uptown hotel, all the artists and radicals and really interesting people stayed there and it was very French." The women
are delighted when Freddy introduces them to people in the dining room.
"They were all names she had heard of or read of in the book columns of
the *Daily News*."

Mark Twain in his old age came to live at 21 Fifth Avenue, a narrow house
on the southeast corner of Fifth Avenue and Ninth Street designed by
James Renwick. Although he lived there only four years, 1904–08, he was
a very noticeable figure in the neighborhood. He had discovered the white
serge suits that he henceforth wore nearly every day. (He claimed that
they were more sanitary than black.) Twain delighted in parading Fifth
Avenue and in being noticed in his striking garb. When he died in 1910,

he was buried from the Brick Presbyterian Church on Thirty-seventh Street and Fifth Avenue. Just a block away from Twain's house was the residential Grosvenor Hotel, on the northeast corner of Tenth Street, where Willa Cather lived in the late 1920s.

Lower Fifth Avenue's literary and artistic associations were endless. In the apartment house at 23 Fifth Avenue reigned Mabel Dodge, a high-brow hostess of ample fortune, who from 1912 or 1913 onward held regular "evenings" in her salon, entertaining writers and artists. Her apartment was decorated all in white: white wallpaper and a white bearskin rug on the floor. Her celebrated circle, which included the anarchist Emma Goldman, the photographer Alfred Stieglitz, and the journalist John Reed, is portrayed in a handsome enamel mural now decorating a wall in the Sheridan Square subway station. The Salmagundi Club, an association of artists founded in 1871 (its name derives from Washington Irving's humorous journal), bought 47 Fifth Avenue, on the east side of Fifth Avenue between Eleventh and Twelfth streets, a brownstone built in 1854 and still used as the clubhouse.

About 1900 the Three Fifth Avenue Club was formed, a sort of cooperative lodging and club for artists and "freethinkers," the catchword then for people who were not so much antiestablishment as *un*establishment. It was at the club that a famous dinner—hosted by Mark Twain—was given in the spring of 1906 for Maxim Gorky, the proletarian writer from Russia, who was much admired by the freethinkers. Gorky was traveling with a lady who, it turned out, was not his wife; there was a Mrs. Gorky, but she had been left behind in Russia. Pulpits were outraged; even the Brevoort refused to take the couple in, "as it would be bad for business." Gorky and companion were forced to take refuge on Staten Island, apparently more liberal than Greenwich Village.

At 1 Fifth Avenue the "A" Club met to promote women's suffrage and "social reform," rather vaguely described in their public statements. Among the members were Mary Heaton Vorse, the journalist; Rose O'Neill, creator of the comic characters the Kewpies; and the social worker Frances Perkins, who later became secretary of labor in President Franklin D. Roosevelt's cabinet.

One of the first and most rousing manifestations of the new Bohemia was "The Republic of Washington Square" in 1916. Gertrude Drick, an artist from Texas who was studying with John Sloan, organized a party to go to the top of the arch: herself, Sloan, the artist Marcel Duchamp, and the actors Forrest Mann, Charles Ellis, and Betty Turner. There is a door and a stairway in the arch and an enclosed space at the top. The party was armed with Chinese lanterns, red balloons, food, much drink, and hot-water bottles. Drick read a declaration proclaiming "the free and independent republic of Washington Square"; the revolutionaries fired off toy pistols, let loose the balloons, and spent the night eating and drinking while an admiring crowd gathered below. John Sloan recorded the event in an etching titled *The Arch Conspirators*. It was never entirely clear what they were rebelling against, but the incident became part of the legend of Greenwich Village. "The Republic of Washington Square" may be said to be the first statement of the square as part of, indeed the capital of, Greenwich Village.

In 1911, when a little-known photographer named Burton Welles progressed along the avenue with his wide-angled camera photographing nearly every building from Washington Square to East Ninety-third Street for his book *Fifth Avenue 1911: New York from Start to Finish*, there were still twenty-four private residences between Washington Square and Fourteenth Street. Between Fourteenth Street and Thirty-fourth Street there were only four, so rapid had been the commercialization of the avenue north of Fourteenth Street. Even the aristocratic survivors on Lower Fifth Avenue had their days numbered. Besieged by the rapidly expanding "Village" to the south and the booming business district to the north, many families finally sold their houses. A number of them settled again on Fifth Avenue, this time above East Fifty-ninth Street, but now in an apartment instead of a house.

In the place of the single-family houses rose large apartment buildings, beginning around the time of World War I and accelerating in the 1920s. The tallest and most striking of these was 1 Fifth Avenue, a twenty-seven-floor luxury apartment building with hotel services built in 1927. It towered over Washington Square, as did an increasing number of high-rise buildings, including those of New York University.

Sentimentalists decried the demolition of the old one-family houses, but, to tell the truth, only a few of them were of any special architectural merit. The dignified charm of the "Knickerbocracy" was lost, but there was a new liveliness in the neighborhood, pleasing in another way. The new residents were often creative and ardent New Yorkers. In a short while, they became as attached to the Lower Fifth Avenue neighborhood as the Knickerbockers had been when it was theirs, and the newcomers, in their turn, were heard to lament any changes.

This photograph of the Grosvenor Hotel, on the northeast corner of Fifth Avenue and Tenth Street, was taken in 1912, when private houses still lined Lower Fifth Avenue. During the following twenty years, large apartment buildings and residential hotels gradually replaced the mansions. Despite these new edifices, Fifth Avenue between Washington Square and Fourteenth Street maintained a sedate architectural presence.

The new buildings on Fifth Avenue between Eighth and Fourteenth streets were mostly on the east side of the street, much of the west side being taken up by the grounds of two great churches, the Church of the Ascension and the First Presbyterian Church. Seventy-five years later most of the apartment houses are still standing. On the whole, they were not nearly so large and elaborate as those built farther up the avenue. They were not family apartments but intended for single people and couples without children. Number 25 on the northeast corner of Ninth Street had apartments as large as six rooms, including a dining room and two baths, but many smaller apartments lacked separate dining rooms. Number 33 on the southeast corner of Tenth Street and number 42 on the southwest corner of Eleventh Street had "dining alcoves." Apartments at number 39 between Tenth and Eleventh streets had a "serving pantry" but no kitchen. Obviously they were intended for bachelors and for bachelorettes, as the new single working women were called, who took their meals in restaurants or ordered them in. The only building with truly grand apartments was number 43 on the northeast corner of Eleventh Street, where the largest apartments had ten rooms and three baths and there were two maids' rooms.

The residents of these new buildings were often notable New Yorkers, not socially prominent as the old town-house families were, but men and women well-known in the city's life. New York governor and 1928 presidential candidate Alfred E. Smith, for instance, lived for years at 51 Fifth Avenue. Judge Joseph Force Crater, the only American to become famous for disappearing, lived in a five-room apartment on the fourth floor of a cooperative building at 40 Fifth Avenue at West Eleventh Street. He was a Tammany Hall Democratic politician who had been rewarded with a justiceship on the New York State Supreme Court. On 3 April 1930 he hailed a cab on West Forty-fifth Street, stepped into it, and was never seen or heard from again. It was a time of judicial scandals, which possibly were connected with the disappearance of Crater, whose reputation for honesty was not immaculate. As the newly founded *Time* magazine remarked, "New York discovered that in addition to judges indicted, judges deposed, and judges jailed, it also had a judge lost."

2

City on the Square

Fourteenth Street to Twenty-third Street

•

Fifth Avenue was cut through to Twenty-third Street as early as 1837, but for some years it intersected only fields and farms. While Fifth Avenue from Washington Square to Fourteenth Street was establishing itself as one of the best residential areas in the city—and soon *the* best area—its route above Fourteenth Street lay through largely vacant land, most of it "common," that is, belonging to the municipality and rented out for farming and for grazing livestock. Much of this common land was uninviting marsh crisscrossed by brooks, and at Fourteenth Street, there was a small pond at which the livestock watered. Mid-island Manhattan was still largely uninhabited. James Fenimore Cooper, in *The American Democrat*, wrote that he could not "remember ever to have seen the immediate environs of so large a town in such a state of general abandonment." To take a stroll in the country the residents of elegant Lower Fifth Avenue had only to walk north a few blocks. Maitland Armstrong, who grew up in Manhattan in the 1850s and later became an artist, recalled, "I have often seen large white sows asleep in the gutter on the corner of 14th Street and 5th."

The future of Fifth Avenue northward depended to a great extent on the development of Madison Square, a large plot of 6.84 acres on the east side of Fifth Avenue between Twenty-third Street and Twenty-sixth Street. In the eighteenth century it was a potter's field; that use was discontinued in 1797. By 1810 it was fenced and trees had been planted. An arsenal and barracks had been built there, a safe distance from the city, necessary because of the stored munitions, which had a habit of exploding. In 1825 the arsenal became a "school," actually a reformatory, called the House of Refuge for the Society for the Protection of Juvenile Delinquents. It was the only building in the square and hardly an attraction for new residents. It burned in 1839, and the city took the opportunity to remove the unfortunate delinquents out of sight to a building at the distant end of East Twenty-third Street. The open space was used as a playing field by the newly organized Knickerbocker Base Ball Club. Madison Square secured a tiny niche in American sports history when, in 1845, the first formal rules for the game were proposed by the Knickerbockers. The square was opened to the public as a park in June 1847, named after President James Madison, whose only connection to New York City was that he once lived very briefly on Cherry Street.

Stagecoaches stopped at Twenty-third Street at a drinking establishment called Madison Cottage, which was embellished with a huge pair of antlers over the door and advertised that coaches departed "every four minutes" for all parts of the city. Rapid service did little for the development of the neighborhood, however: riding a stage was expensive, and few downtowners were inclined to spend the money to reach dusty Madison Square for recreation. Then there was the city's livestock market just north of Twenty-third Street. It was serviced by the Bull's Head Tavern, a cattleman's saloon, nearby. In 1850 the market was moved north to Forty-second Street, then still farther north to East Ninety-fourth Street as that neighborhood developed, and, finally, in the 1880s to the Jersey shore.

The open space of Madison Square and its enviable position at the junction of Fifth Avenue and Broadway invited development despite the unpromising surroundings. The reformatory disappeared, then the taverns and the livestock, and new houses, spacious and stately, began to line the north and east sides of the square opposite Fifth Avenue; their addresses were Madison Square East or Madison Square North, it being considered more select—with overtones of London sophistication—to have an address on a square rather than a numbered street. Members of the Stokes, Schieffelin, Ronalds, and Wolfe families, rich and socially well-known, built large houses in the new neighborhood.

On Fifth Avenue itself between Fourteenth and Twenty-third streets splendid houses, most of them fronted with brownstone, continued to rise. When the *New York Herald* published a list of the city's two hundred richest men in 1851, half already lived north of Fourteenth Street. More of them lived on Fifth Avenue than on any other street; already it was the best address. In 1882 James D. McCabe, Jr., wrote in his unblushing account of the city, *New York by Sunlight and Gaslight*, "To live and die in a Fifth Avenue mansion is the dearest wish of every New Yorker's heart. Though the lower squares are being rapidly encroached upon by business edifices, the street as a whole maintains its character as the most magnificent avenue of residences in the world."

One of the finest houses was built by Marshall O. Roberts, who before the Civil War made an enormous fortune from government subsidies for mail carried by his steamship lines. During the war he sold his decrepit vessels to the federal government for military use. Several promptly sank on reaching deep water. There was a scandal, but Roberts was politically well-connected and ended up making even more money. His home on the avenue at Eighteenth Street was enriched with costly European and American paintings, most of them by living artists. At receptions, the house was darkened except for the picture gallery, brightly lighted by gas. In the place of honor hung Emanuel Leutze's already celebrated painting *Washington Crossing the Delaware*, surrounded by the works of Albert Bierstadt, Frederic Edwin Church, and Rosa Bonheur. Then, as now, patronage of art was an almost certain path into social prominence. Roberts and his wife were accepted in spite of the dubious origins of his fortune and became as noted for their hospitality as for their art collection.

In the 1880s Madison Square and Fifth Avenue were considered the most attractive part of the city. James McCabe could call the square "the prettiest of all the smaller parks of New York.... It is well shaded by noble

trees, and fairly smiles with gay flowers in the summer. A fine fountain in the centre is one of its chief attractions, and around it gather, on fair mornings, crowds of children and nurses from the neighboring fashionable streets." The fashionableness of Madison Square was subtly different from that of Washington Square, showier and less aloof. Nobody ever called the residents of *this* square cave dwellers. Madison Square developed most rapidly in the post–Civil War years first called the Gilded Age by Mark Twain. Men interested in "sport," which meant the equestrian sports, lived around the square. One of their leaders was Leonard Jerome, whose house was on Twenty-sixth Street and Madison Avenue. A Wall Street operator of varying fortune, Jerome was mad for sports, a yachtsman, a four-in-hand coach driver, and owner of racehorses. In 1866, he

The shipowner Marshall O. Roberts was one of the first to build a grand house on Fifth Avenue above Fourteenth Street. The double residence on the southeast corner of Fifth Avenue and Eighteenth Street boasted an extensive art gallery, Roberts being a major collector and patron of living artists. The house was demolished around 1895 to make room for a commercial building.

and the American Jockey Club promoted a racetrack in the Bronx named in his honor, Jerome Park, where the Belmont Stakes were run until the track closed in 1889.

The poet laureate of Madison Square was a New York lawyer named William Allen Butler, living on West Twelfth Street, who amused himself by writing light verse for magazines. In 1857 he published in *Harper's Weekly* a poem satirizing the social ambitions of the local swells entitled "Miss Flora M'Flimsey of Madison Square." This long piece of doggerel was the lament of a fashionable young lady who tirelessly bought new clothes in New York and Paris yet had "nothing to wear."

At the end of the poem Flora is exhausted by shopping but still dissatisfied with her wardrobe:

> And yet, though scarce three months have passed since the day
> This merchandise went, on twelve carts, up Broadway,
> The same Miss M'Flimsey, of Madison Square,
> The last time we met was in utter despair,
> Because she had nothing whatever to wear!

To the surprise of its author, the poem was an immediate success: *Harper's* sold eighty thousand copies of the issue containing it, an extraordinary number for the time; newspapers everywhere picked the poem up and reprinted it—without paying royalties, so the dismayed author received only his original fifty-dollar fee from the magazine. "Miss Flora M'Flimsey" was published as a book in both New York and London and regarded everywhere as a biting satire on the idle and spendthrift New Yorkers; for years the poem was a byword for social pretension and excess. William Dean Howells, the most prominent American literary critic of the day, surprisingly declared that the poem "deserved a permanent place in literature."

The Fifth Avenue Presbyterian Church, which counted many Madison Square residents among its congregation, was built on the southeast corner of Fifth Avenue and Nineteenth Street in 1852–53; the architect was Leopold Eidlitz, who designed other religious structures in the city. The subsequent history of the church was unusual: in 1875 it was sold at auction and presented by the buyer to the Central Presbyterian Church, which dismantled the building and re-erected it again on West Fifty-seventh Street.

At Eighteenth Street from 1859 stood the Episcopal Church of St. Ann's, whose special field of Christian endeavor was deaf-mutes. In 1893 there were more than one hundred deaf-mute communicants, ministered to by Dr. Thomas Gallaudet, member of a family famous for its devotion to education for the deaf. The South Reformed Dutch Church was built on the southwest corner of Fifth Avenue and Twenty-first Street in 1849 and remained there until 1890.

Madison Square had neither the aristocratic cachet of Lower Fifth Avenue nor its feeling of neighborhood; commerce intruded too soon. It was home, however, to many of the city's fashionable clubs at a time when club life—that is, men's club life—was of great importance in the city. In the latter half of the nineteenth century most gentlemen belonged to at least one club. By the last quarter of the century there were more than a hundred clubs in New York City with a total membership of over fifty thousand; among the great cities of the world only London had more clubmen.

Preeminent was the Union Club, founded in 1836. In 1855 it moved to Fifth Avenue and Twenty-first Street from Broadway, another sign of the abandonment of that avenue for the more stylish Fifth Avenue. The new Union Club, which cost around three hundred thousand dollars, was described as the first building in New York designed exclusively as a clubhouse. In the 1870s the Union, with membership limited to one thousand, was generally supposed to be the richest club in the world.

James Gordon Bennett, the outspoken Scottish-born founder of the *New York Herald,* was a sulfurous critic of most New York institutions, and wrote dismissively of the Union, "Will it promote principle, taste, philosophy, talent and genius? It may aid cooking, eating, and conversational powers, but one hour of solitary bliss of true genius is worth an eternity of meretricious social happiness." Bennett could afford to be sarcastic: he was so scorned by society as a low newspaperman that he would never be asked to join *any* club. His *Herald* was a sensational sheet that shocked (but titillated) the public by accepting advertisements for prostitutes,

Founded in 1836, the Union Club moved in 1855 from its home on Broadway to the northwest corner of Fifth Avenue and Twenty-first Street. The initiation fee in 1876 was $300 and the annual dues were $75; military officers were exempt from the annual dues. In 1903 the club moved to the northeast corner of Fifth Avenue and Fifty-first Street since by that time most of its members lived "uptown." It is now at Park Avenue and Sixty-ninth Street.

even putting them on the front page. He also used the plain description *legs* instead of the customary *limbs* and even *pants* instead of *unmentionables*. His fellow editors and rivals professed to despise him, although envy of his success obviously featured in their detestation. Among the terms they used to describe Bennett were *infidel, venal wretch, pestilential scoundrel, habitual liar,* and the simple but effective *turkey buzzard.* Conservative New Yorkers contrasted the *Herald* with the *New York Post,* a stately but prissy daily. One New York society matron, Mrs. Frederick P. Bellamy, explained the depravity of New York by asking, "What can you expect of a city in which every morning the *Herald* makes vice attractive, and every night the *Post* makes virtue odious?"

James Gordon Bennett, Jr., heir to the *Herald*, was an enthusiastic club-man—he joined about a dozen—although he was soon asked to resign from many of them. Immensely rich and irritatingly self-confident, he had a racy sense of humor and was quite uninhibited. He was also a notable drinker. At the Union Club in the 1870s the younger Bennett introduced a new sport called Bennetting. Near the clubhouse on Fifth Avenue were a number of refined academies for the education of young ladies. A pro-cession of demure girls being taken out for a walk, led, of course, by chap-erones, was a familiar sight in New York, so much so that Winslow Homer did a drawing in 1868 for *Harper's Weekly* entitled *The Morning Walk— Young Ladies School Promenading the Avenue,* which showed boarding school girls taking their after-breakfast walk along Fifth Avenue at Madison Square. Most days, Bennett was on the watch from the windows of the Union Club, where he generally boozed in the afternoons. He would rush out of the club and shriekingly dash through the line, scat-tering the schoolgirls amid shrill cries of dismay and, no doubt, delicious excitement. This adolescent sport, imitated by other raucous members of the club, was, in a day when young girls were cherished, regarded as scan-dalous in the extreme. As one of Bennett's biographers coolly remarked, the Union "was obviously no intellectual citadel."

The Union Club was followed into the neighborhood by the Athenaeum, Manhattan, Lotos, Travellers', and Arcadian clubs. Most of these made their headquarters in modified town houses, as only the rich Union had the money to build its own clubhouse. At number 96, on the southwest corner of Fifteenth Street, stood an elaborate house, said to have cost one hundred thousand dollars, belonging to Mrs. Charles Maverick Parker, that in 1865 became the home of the Manhattan Club. This was the headquarters of the "Swallow Tail Democracy," bluntly described by James McCabe as "the better elements" of the Democratic party. The swallowtail was a dress coat not usually worn by the rough-and-ready Democrats who frequented Tammany Hall. In a day when a gentleman

A major industry in nine-teenth-century New York was the manufacture and sale of musical instruments. Piano makers often built recital halls in which to display their products, and one of the finest was Chickering Hall (near left in photo), built in 1875 on the northwest corner of Fifth Avenue and Eighteenth Street. Besides concerts, the hall was also a popular venue for lectures and art auctions until it closed in 1893.

might make one or more regular stops between office and home, all these clubs were on his regular route. Many members dined at one of their clubs and stayed there when their families were out of town and the servants on vacation.

On the northwest corner of Fifth Avenue and Eighteenth Street the Chickering Piano Company opened Chickering Hall in 1875. It was a showroom for their products (the other great New York piano company, Steinway and Sons, had one, too, on East Fourteenth Street) and was rented out for concerts and public events of a dignified nature. It was here in 1876 that Alexander Graham Bell gave a demonstration of his telephone during which his select audience heard the hymn *In the Sweet Bye and Bye* sung in New Brunswick, New Jersey, transmitted over thirty-two miles of telegraph wires to Chickering Hall.

A small hotel on Fifth Avenue across Eighteenth Street was the Hotel de Logerot, formerly the mansion of Gordon W. Burnham. *King's Handbook* of 1893 called it "very fashionable and very aristocratic, and the landlord is a genuine nobleman, Richard de Logerot, Marquis de Croisic, who has a good standing in New York's 'Four Hundred'." His title was used for an apartment hotel built in 1887 on the northwest corner of Fifth Avenue and Twenty-sixth Street called the Croisic.

Hotels clustered around the important intersection formed by Twenty-third Street, Broadway, and Fifth Avenue. Already, New York's avenues had distinctive characters: "Broadway crosses Fifth Avenue," wits said, "but never runs side by side." Broadway was busier, noisier, flashier, more commercial than Fifth Avenue and always more of an entertainment center. Fifth Avenue never had theaters as Broadway did; the well-known Fifth Avenue Theatre was not actually on the avenue but slightly off it on Twenty-sixth Street. However, like clubs, hotels flourished there.

At the northeast corner of Fifth Avenue and Twenty-sixth Street stood the Brunswick Hotel, used as headquarters by the rich sporting fraternity of the neighborhood. It was famous as the meeting place of the Coaching Club, dedicated to the difficult art of four-in-hand, that is, driving a coach drawn by four horses. The club started its famous annual parades up Fifth Avenue at the Hotel Brunswick. These were great crowd pleasers from 1876 to 1903, by which time there were too many automobiles on the avenue for a stately parade of horses. The Brunswick Hotel was famous for its cooking and was the chosen place for the multiple-course dinners given by the Coaching Club and other sporting groups.

In 1853 a major amusement spot, Franconi's Hippodrome, opened on the northwest corner of Fifth Avenue and Twenty-third Street, where Broadway intersected Fifth Avenue. This huge arena seated about six thousand people with room for three thousand standees. The structure was rather an immense tent than a building. Pageants with elephants and camels, chariot races, and gladiatorial contests in keeping with the Roman name were staged there for two seasons, but the enterprise was not a financial success. The building was torn down in 1856, when the site was taken for the Fifth Avenue Hotel.

One of the legendary hotels in American history, the Fifth Avenue received its first guests in 1859. A white marble building six stories tall, it had a remarkable six hundred rooms, holding about eight hundred guests. More than a hundred suites had a parlor, a bedchamber, a dressing room, and a bath. It boasted a "vertical railroad," or elevator, the first installed in a hotel in the United States (though preceded by elevators in a few office buildings). "A new and admirable feature," the *Home Journal* told its fascinated readers, "consists of steam elevators in various parts of the building, which will be constantly moving up and down from the first to the sixth floor, thereby rendering the higher suits [sic] of apartments as eligible to families as those lower down. Ladies need no more dread the fatigue incident to going up and down stairs...."

The elevator was a great instrument of change in the perception of guests: in the past, rooms on the lower floors had been the most desirable because easier to reach. The upper floors were always cheaper; at the top and least desirable were the servants' rooms. Before the advent of the elevator the idea of an inviting view as an advantage in living accommodations was almost unknown. After the installation of elevators in hotels and, later, in residential buildings, the higher floors, rising above the noise and dust of the streets and affording relaxing vistas, immediately became the most desirable and expensive lodgings.

When the Fifth Avenue Hotel opened, a guest could obtain a room in a good location and four meals (breakfast, lunch, dinner, and tea) for two dollars and fifty cents a day. The hotel, like most in New York City, was run on the "American" plan, with all meals included in the daily rate. Guests were generally all served at one sitting in the immense dining room. Tea, a light meal, was served some hours after the four or five o'clock dinner, which was the main meal of the day and in hotels an exceedingly copious one. Foreign visitors marveled at the length of American hotel menus, as indeed they marveled at the size, splendor, and service of the hotels themselves. The sheer number of hotels in the city staggered Europeans and Americans both; by 1870 New York had at least six hundred.

The Fifth Avenue Hotel advertised accommodations for families because, like most hotels in nineteenth-century New York, it catered to long-term

When the Fifth Avenue Hotel opened in 1859 at the intersection of Fifth Avenue, Broadway, and Twenty-third Street, the neighborhood was the smartest meeting place in New York, as O. Henry acknowledged when he said, "Spin it on a pivot, and you see the world." When this photograph was taken in 1894, life still swirled around the hotel, though by then it had begun to enter its decline. In 1908, after more than half a century as New York's best-known hotel, the Fifth Avenue Hotel was demolished and replaced by an office building.

The public rooms of the Fifth Avenue Hotel were well furnished, but not nearly so overstuffed as those in hotels built later on Fifth Avenue. The hotel was large even by today's standards, with a staff of four hundred and accomodations for eight hundred guests. Its high standards of service greatly impressed foreign visitors, who also noted the number of people, including families with children, who lived permanently in the hotel.

residents as well as transient guests. Charles Dickens, among other travelers, was struck by the number of families who lived permanently in hotels in New York. Newlyweds, in particular, were likely to spend the first year or two of their married life in a hotel—a boardinghouse, really, since the management provided all meals—before establishing their own home. Setting up housekeeping was an expensive step since it involved furnishing a house and hiring a staff of servants. Some visitors thought the excellence of New York hotels was due to the fact that they operated with this basis of permanent patronage.

The Eno family, a New York real-estate dynasty, owned the Fifth Avenue Hotel, but the name most associated with its style was that of the manager Paran Stevens. An experienced hotelier who owned the Revere and Tremont House hotels in Boston, he also built an apartment house on Fifth Avenue at Seventeenth Street that later became the Hotel Victoria. Stevens became a prominent New Yorker of his day. Running a hotel was no barrier to social prominence in New York; the preeminent Astors owned several.

It was just as well that there was no social barrier to hotel proprietorship since Paran Stevens's wife assuredly had social aspirations. New York society did not quite know what to make of Mrs. Stevens. She was an indefatigable partygoer and hostess, given to wearing the most extreme fashions and to redecorating her house in an increasingly stately style with oversize statuary and potted palms without number. She entertained at home at 244 Fifth Avenue near Twenty-seventh Street with solemn musicales noted as much for the frugal refreshments as for the performances. A guest once told her frankly that he had certainly come for the pleasure of seeing her since otherwise he got nothing but a cup of cold tea.

Paran Stevens died in 1872, and his widow moved uptown to 1 East Fifty-seventh Street, in the "Marble Row" houses built by Mary Mason Jones, where she pursued social laurels even more ardently. She succeeded in marrying her daughter Mary Fiske ("Minnie") Stevens to Almeric Hugh Paget, member of a titled English family. Minnie became famous in London as the sponsor of American debutantes being presented to the queen at Buckingham Palace. (Americans had to have an English sponsor of acceptable social standing.) Her rivals insinuated that Minnie took fees for this service, and she probably did, but she became one of the best-known Americans in London. There was a Stevens son, too, who was once engaged to marry Edith Newbold Jones, later the novelist Edith Wharton.

Until 1908, when it was torn down and replaced by an office building, the Fifth Avenue Hotel had a special place in New York life. As Mabel Osgood Wright said in her memoirs of a New York childhood, it was a place of "respectable revelry and testimonial banquets." Politicians, largely Republican, gathered at its men's bar. The state Republican Party had its headquarters in the hotel, and most days in the 1880s the Republican boss U.S. Senator Thomas C. Platt, could be seen in the bar, surrounded by office seekers. Petitioners gathered in the so-called Amen Corner, a corridor off the lobby, and when Platt conferred with his colleagues, wits called the meetings Platt's Sunday School Class. It was at one of these confabulations in 1898 that Theodore Roosevelt was nominated for the governorship of New York.

The *Evening Post* declared that the opening of the Fifth Avenue Hotel gave impetus for businesses to open on Fifth Avenue up to Twenty-third Street. Residents were annoyed and appalled. Clubs and first-class hotels were not detrimental to quiet neighborhood life, but shops were. Such upper-class Americans of the nineteenth century as lived on Fifth Avenue did not want "trade" next door, a great change from eighteenth-century New York, when the best people had lived above the shop. Retail establishments and services, along with stables, had been confined to the side streets off Fifth Avenue, to Sixth Avenue, or to Broadway. Especially offensive to Fifth Avenue were shop signboards publicly proclaiming their low occupations. Neighbors' protests were the first skirmishes in the long-running battle over commercial signage that still rages along Fifth Avenue.

In 1859 the family of young Brander Matthews, later a playwright and professor of drama at Columbia University, settled at 101 Fifth Avenue, on the east side of the avenue between Seventeenth and Eighteenth streets. "When we moved into 101…there was not a shop of any kind anywhere up and down the length of the stately street," he wrote in his *Reminiscences*. "So hostile was the sentiment of the dwellers on the avenue toward the invasion of trade that it must have taken desperate courage for the first shopkeeper to intrude into the consecrated region."

Lord & Taylor, founded in 1826, was a flourishing dry goods store when well-to-do households were beginning to build on Fifth Avenue. The main store was on "Ladies' Mile" at the southwest corner of Broadway and Twentieth Street; a branch for cheaper goods was on Grand Street. In 1871, the store expanded and moved to the building pictured, on the southeast corner of Fifth Avenue and Nineteenth Street. In 1914, Lord & Taylor moved to its present location on the northwest corner of Fifth Avenue and Thirty-eighth Street.

A tailor with the felicitous name G. D. Happy was the brave man. His irate neighbors muttered that if the business should fail, "he wouldn't be so God-Dammed happy." Alas, the tailor prospered, and other businesses followed. A part-time poet named George Arnold was moved to write, mournfully, that Fifth Avenue was "falling from grace...."

In 1871, Dunlap and Co. opened a store at Fifth Avenue and Twenty-third Street. The entire building was devoted to clothing: retail on the street, tailors on the second floor, milliners and dressmakers on the floors above. Alarmed by the advance of trade, prominent families began to desert the Madison Square neighborhood. They did not desert Fifth Avenue; however, most of them moving up to the "better" neighborhoods of Fifth Avenue in the Thirties and Forties. A few ventured north of Forty-second Street. Freestanding mansions, such as the Marshall O. Roberts and August Belmont houses, were torn down, and the neighborhood began to fill up with piano warehouses and furniture stores. "One is in the land of the practical," an observer lamented.

There was no halting commerce, and little municipal zoning in those days protected neighborhoods. Stately houses on sites suitable for business fell before high offers. In 1867 ex-mayor George Opdyke's house on Fifth Avenue near Sixteenth Street was sold to James A. Hearn and Son for their department store at the record price of $105,000. Opdyke himself had been a dry-goods merchant and importer but had kept his own shop downtown.

After the first *Social Register* appeared in 1887, it became a popular sport of newspaper writers to try to locate the "social center of New York," which was arrived at by determining which neighborhood had the most residents listed in the book and then locating the center of that neighborhood. In 1888 the social center of New York was Fifth Avenue and Twenty-first Street.

Apartment buildings first appeared on Fifth Avenue about the same time as shops. The first was the Richard K. Haight family house at Fifteenth Street, which was converted in 1871 to twenty "family" apartments on four floors, each renting for from two to three thousand dollars a year (New York rents then, and until the 1940s, were quoted in annual terms), with fifteen "bachelor apartments" on the fifth floor. The building advertised an elevator, an "internal telegraph," and a restaurant, as well as housekeeping service for the bachelors since it assumed that they were unable to do anything domestic for themselves.

Bachelor flats were a great success; soon entire buildings only for bachelors were being constructed in this and other prime residential neighborhoods. They were especially dense on Fifth Avenue a few blocks north of Madison Square. Masculine celibates, as the newspapers coyly called them, were the object of much curiosity; for most of the latter half of the nineteenth century, New York had a surplus of unmarried men. At a time when most men married directly from the family home, those who remained single for years and even set up housekeeping on their own were a new phenomenon, as the press tirelessly reminded its readers, and fascinated the public.

Bachelor apartments usually contained a parlor, a bedroom, and a bath, the rooms generally in a row in that order. They rarely had a vestibule or hall: you stepped directly into the parlor. Breakfast was served from a central kitchen in the building; other meals were taken in restaurants or sent in.

An invitation to a meal in a bachelor apartment was thrilling to female hearts, which seemed to have pictured debauchery as the rule in bachelor flats. Accompanied by a chaperone, the ladies were given unusual, bachelorish things to eat, such as a mixed grill or a Welsh rarebit, or game and oysters, which were thought to be "male" foods. References to these bachelor apartments in literature loved to play on the name *Benedict,* after the long-time bachelor in *Much Ado about Nothing.* In Mrs. Burton Harrison's 1890 novel *The Anglomaniacs,* we meet the bachelor Dick Huntley, "who lived in the Benedick, with his violoncello and a pair of dachshunds."

Apartments like this rented for around one thousand dollars a year; it was computed that an unmarried man with an annual income of five thousand dollars (a substantial upper middle-class figure) could live very comfortably in such a flat. A writer in a 1900 issue of the *New-York Daily Tribune* was made uncomfortable at the thought of all this comfort and ease for solitary males: "These homes for bachelors are so attractively designed that they are likely to bring about a marked reduction in wedding statistics….When over and above the fascinations of the clubs in Fifth-ave. and elsewhere bachelors find it easy to rent apartments so sumptuous and so cunningly contrived as to shut out all thoughts of family life, is it not plain that the outlook is somewhat dispiriting?"

There were still plenty of families around Madison Square at the turn of the century, when it was known to most New Yorkers for its baby carriages, since a favorite spot of nurses from the town houses around the park was to parade their charges in the latest-style perambulators. Another familiar Madison Square sight was a row of hansom cabs on the Fifth Avenue side waiting for passengers. The Fifth Avenue line was owned by Elliott F. Shepard, who was married to a granddaughter of Commodore Vanderbilt. He was religious and severe, "and the number one rule of the line," wrote Hurlbert Footner, "was that any driver who used bad language would immediately be discharged. It was supposed that Mr. Shepard had placed spotters up and down the route to make sure that the rule was obeyed."

In 1902 the George A. Fuller Building was erected on the triangular site where the St. Germain Hotel had stood, bounded by Fifth Avenue, Broadway, and East Twenty-second Street. The building, designed by Daniel H. Burnham to fit the odd site (called by a wit "a stingy piece of pie"), became one of the most admired in New York, but first reactions were not especially approving: it created a wind tunnel that sent hats flying and skirts billowing, and some nervous commentators feared that the slender edifice might fall over and crush the neighborhood. Several years passed before New Yorkers realized that the distinctive building had enriched the cityscape. Charles Hanson Towne, then a young man, wrote of the so-called Flatiron, "The wonder of it! We stood in awe before the strange shape, admiring or considering its lines, saying 'What next? What next in this strange town of ours?'" There was a social reverberation, too; the building of the Flatiron emphasized the increasingly commercial atmosphere of the district. *The WPA Guide to New York City* said, "Completion of the Fuller Building presaged the end of Madison Square as a social center."

In the meantime, manufacturing, especially of clothing, regarded as even more detrimental to the neighborhood than retailing, was creeping in, moving northwest from the Lower East Side, where it had begun as piecework done at home in tenement houses. Madison Square became the center of the garment industry by 1910. By 1915, Fifth Avenue from Fourteenth Street to Twenty-third Street was largely the home of wholesale trade and garment manufacturing. Its density was astounding: in April 1915 a census counted 491 garment factories employing 51,476 hands in the area. Showrooms were opened in old residential buildings.

The George A. Fuller Building, more famously known as the Flatiron Building, was built in 1903. The intersection at the top of the triangular site was one of the most heavily trafficked in New York. At bottom right is the Fifth Avenue Hotel.

In 1923 Robert Cortes Holliday, a magazine editor, wrote with distaste of "furniture auctioneers…chain stores, buffet lunches, self-service, and automat restaurants" in the neighborhood, and of "that mammoth spectacle of frowsiness at the noon hour: the dense promenade of hordes and hordes of unkempt, alien-tongue garment workers on this once patrician pavement!"

Considering its size, the garment industry had an amazingly short life around Madison Square. The Fifth Avenue Association got busy lobbying, and in the next ten years managed by skillful use of zoning laws to relocate the garment district farther north and west to Seventh Avenue in the Thirties. Madison Square, however, never recovered either as a residential area or as clubland. It remained dedicated to business even though the retail trade was steadily moving up Fifth Avenue. By World War I, Fifth Avenue shops in the vicinity of Madison Square included Park & Tilford, for fancy groceries; Mark Cross, for harness and leather goods; Brentano's, for books; Peck & Peck, for hosiery; and E. B. Meyrowitz, for optical ware. Many of these were household names in New York for decades to come.

The second most famous disappearance (after Judge Crater) in New York City's history occurred here. On 12 December 1910 an Upper East Side debutante named Dorothy Arnold stopped into the Brentano's shop on Fifth Avenue and Twenty-seventh Street, bought a "light novel," ran into a friend at the corner, chatted, and then walked up Fifth Avenue into oblivion. Her family did not inform the police for six weeks. They apparently suspected a man in the case, although they denied this. Her father theorized that Dorothy had been murdered by "garroters" and her body thrown into the reservoir in Central Park. In any event, she was never heard from again.

Even as late as 1917 the intersection of Fifth Avenue and Twenty-third Street was one of the busiest corners in New York. A survey made by the police in that year showed that during business hours, 8:30 A.M. to 6:30 P.M., 159,920 pedestrians and 9,645 vehicles passed the corner. This was a much different traffic pattern from the intersection at Fifth Avenue and Forty-second Street, where there were fewer pedestrians, 113,780, but many more vehicles, 18,000. In pedestrian count, both of these intersections were still far behind the busiest corner in the city, at Park Row and Frankfurt Street in the financial district downtown, where 296,200 pedestrians but hardly any vehicles passed during those ten hours.

For a brief period, but only a brief period, Madison Square was central to New York City's public life. By the late nineteenth century the square was midpoint in a developed Fifth Avenue. When funds were being raised in 1885 to build a base for the Statue of Liberty, the immense arm of "Miss Liberty" was shipped from France and displayed in the square to arouse interest and raise funds by demonstrating the colossal size of the statue. The sculptor, Frédéric Bartholdi, was commemorated in the name of a hotel on East Twenty-third Street.

On the east side of the square, on the blockfront between East Twenty-sixth and Twenty-seventh streets, stood first a railroad station for the New York Central line, then, between 1879 and 1889, the first Madison Square Garden, where circuses, concerts, pageants, and horse shows were held. In 1890 a grand building, designed by McKim, Mead & White in the Venetian Renaissance style, opened with a restaurant, a roof garden, and a concert hall as well as a coliseum, all surmounted by a tower with its infamous *Diana*. The new Madison Square Garden immediately became one of the most popular places of public entertainment in the city, until it, in turn, was demolished in 1925.

In 1892 two temporary arches were erected over Fifth Avenue, one at Twenty-second Street, designed by Stanford White, the other at Fifty-ninth Street, as a setting for a great parade celebrating the four hundredth anniversary of Columbus's discovery of America. Between Twenty-second and Thirty-fourth streets the imaginative White erected one hundred poles, each sixty feet high, topped with eagles and other patriotic devices, and lighted by Venetian lights to form a stunning setting for the celebrations. White arranged it all from the nearby office of McKim, Mead & White at 1 West Twentieth Street, the northwest corner of Fifth Avenue. Two years later the firm, by then the largest architectural firm in the world, moved to the Mohawk Building at 160 Fifth Avenue, the southwest corner of Twenty-first Street.

The eyes of all New York and even of the entire United States were on Madison Square in 1899, when Commodore George Dewey, naval hero of the Spanish–American War and victor in the battle with the Spanish fleet in Manila Bay, was honored by a great parade up Fifth Avenue. The country had gone temporarily crazy over this hitherto undistinguished and unpretentious admiral. Clippings from newspapers that had sung Dewey's praises during the months since his victory were gathered together and presented to him in a volume that weighed one hundred fifty pounds and was bound in solid silver. New York City joyfully received

Dewey with a naval review, a parade of ships up the Hudson River, and on 30 September a parade up Fifth Avenue by the U.S. Army and Navy and the New York State Militia.

An extraordinary arch more than a hundred feet tall made of "staff," a mixture of wood shavings and plaster painted white that well simulated marble, spanned Fifth Avenue just above Twenty-third Street. Modeled, at least distantly, on the Arch of Titus in Rome and resembling the Arc de Triômphe in Paris, the design was modified to include naval references: a chariot drawn by four seahorses called *Naval Victory* and sculptures of previous American naval heroes such as John Paul Jones.

In the first flush of enthusiasm there was an announcement that the arch was to be reproduced in permanent marble and granite, like Washington Square Arch, then under construction. Subscriptions were solicited. They arrived but slowly, as memories of the little war faded. The cost was estimated at five hundred thousand dollars; less than half that was raised. A year later the staff was flaking rapidly, and the triumphal arch was a peeling eyesore. It was then given to the city of Charleston, planning an international exposition for 1902. Some of the sculptured figures were used in the fairgrounds, and then, surprisingly, the city of Charleston managed to lose the arch, which has never reappeared.

From 1911 to World War II a community Christmas was celebrated in Madison Square with an enormous tree and carols. The party was the idea of an artist named Orlando Rouland and his wife. This was about the last manifestation of community spirit in the square; there were now too few residents to support such a festivity.

In 1918, at the end of World War I, John F. Hylan, who had risen from the position of motorman on one of the elevated rail lines in the city to mayor as the protégé of newspaper publisher William Randolph Hearst and was not regarded as one of New York's most able chief executives, promoted a Victory Arch to honor the city's war dead, which was executed in temporary materials at a cost of eighty thousand dollars by Thomas Hastings, architect with John M. Carrère of the New York Public Library. Like the Dewey Triumphal and Memorial Arch, it was modeled on a Roman arch, Constantine's. Busy sculpture honored not only the military

After winning the Battle of Manila Bay during the Spanish-American War in 1898, George Dewey, a modest naval officer put in command of the Asiatic squadron by Theodore Roosevelt (then secretary of the navy), was promoted to admiral and enthusiastically feted upon his return to the United States in 1899. His grandest reception was in New York, where he surveyed a miles-long parade in his honor from an arch bridging Fifth Avenue at Madison Square, shown here. Subscriptions were solicited to erect a permanent marble arch, but Dewey's popularity faded fast, and with it plans for his monument.

but also civilian workers in the war. Again, a permanent marble version was to be built, but advocates could agree neither on an architect nor a design, and the temporary arch had to be destroyed.

In 1927 it was Charles A. Lindbergh who was honored on his return from his celebrated Atlantic flight. Four million people, believed by historians to be the biggest crowd ever to witness a parade in New York City, lined Fifth Avenue when Lindbergh rode up it in an open car, accompanied by an honor guard of fifteen thousand soldiers and preceded by a chariot containing three women dressed in flowing white gowns blowing golden trumpets. At Twenty-third Street the parade halted for Lindbergh to lay a wreath on the Eternal Light, placed in Madison Square to honor the dead of World War I.

3
Cosmopolitan Arrival

Twenty-third Street to Thirty-fourth Street

•

When William B. Astor, Jr., built a four-story brick house with brownstone trim on the southwest corner of Fifth Avenue and Thirty-fourth Street in 1856 and his brother John Jacob III built next door on the northeast corner of Fifth Avenue and Thirty-third Street two years later— a garden separated the houses—it was a signal that society was moving uptown on Fifth Avenue. Previously, various members of the Astor family had clustered around Lafayette Street, well to the east of Fifth Avenue. However, that neighborhood was growing unfashionable, and at the same time the younger generation of the family, especially the women, were growing socially ambitious.

The new Astor houses were neither imposing nor large by the later standards of Fifth Avenue, but they were admired. An 1859 newspaper described John Jacob's house as "a mansion presenting a rather unique appearance…. It is faced with Philadelphia brick, and the window dressings, architraves, cornices, rustic columns, and stoop are made of Nova Scotia freestone." Another mark of distinction was the mansard roof, an innovation that immediately became popular with New Yorkers.

Across Thirty-fourth Street on the northwest corner of Fifth Avenue stood the brownstone house of Dr. Samuel B. Townsend. Townsend was a monarch of patent medicine who had invented a "Compound Extract of Sarsaparilla" that was immediately successful and made him a millionaire. Sarsaparilla is an extract of greenbriar plants much used in the nineteenth century for medicinal purposes and also for popular soft drinks. Dr. Townsend advertised in *The Police Gazette* and similar publications and did not hesitate to make wide claims for his extract, which was said to cure "dyspepsia, scrofula, tumors, and cancers," among other afflictions. The advertisements were packed with personal testimonials from customers describing rapid cures of the most serious and debilitating sicknesses after drinking a bottle or two of Sarsaparilla.

On the site of Dr. Townsend's house, which was demolished after his death, in 1864, rose the marble palace—for it could hardly be called a house—of Alexander Turney Stewart and his wife, Cornelia, built between 1864 and 1869. The Astors across the street were socially unaware of their neighbor. In the social stratification of the time there was a wide gap between fortunes derived from land and those derived from "trade." The Astors were considered landed, despite the fact that their land was city real estate, whereas A. T. Stewart owned a department store, the largest and finest of its kind in the United States, but still a shop. He was, therefore, "in trade." He was an Irish immigrant who had opened his first dry-goods shop on Broadway in 1823. By 1862 he had built an "iron palace" on Broadway between Ninth and Tenth streets, one of the largest iron structures in existence, where he did fifty million dollars a year in business, mostly in feminine attire, or, more precisely, in the materials for feminine attire since one bought fabric for making garments rather than "ready to wear," which was almost unknown.

His Fifth Avenue house, which had its long side on West Thirty-fourth Street, was an extraordinary creation for a childless couple (their three children predeceased them) who seldom, if ever, entertained—fifty-five rooms, many of them lined with marble. The ceilings, even in the bedrooms, were nearly nineteen feet high. Every room was a thicket of rosewood furniture with tufted upholstery and bric-a-brac. Although there was an art gallery, the Stewarts' vast collection of paintings (at least 179

Alexander Turney Stewart was the most successful retailer in America by the end of the Civil War. Detested by his employees for his stinginess, Stewart was equally well known for his personal frugality, so it is surprising that he and his wife were the most palatially housed couple in New York. Their fifty-five-room marble house, on the northwest corner of Fifth Avenue and Thirty-fourth Street, was completed in 1869 and demolished around 1900.

Across from the Stewart house stood the house of Mr. and Mrs. William B. Astor, Jr., built in 1856. The Astors' comfortable and well arranged brownstone appeared somewhat insignificant when compared to the Stewarts' colossal marble edifice across Thirty-fourth Street. There were no friendly visits—the Astors looked down on the Stewarts because the latter were "in trade" while the Astors were "in property."

works, many of them of colossal size), white marble statuary, and bronzes overflowed into every room. When wall space ran out, paintings were angled against easels and even on the floor against statues. The majority of the paintings were works of the "modern French school," painted around the middle of the nineteenth century, when Stewart was buying art for his house. He was usually the first owner and, in fact, was a major patron of contemporary art, as many of his Fifth Avenue successors have been.

The most famous painting was Rosa Bonheur's immense *The Horse Fair*, which sold for fifty-three thousand dollars at the auction of the Stewart collection held after Mrs. Stewart's death; Cornelius Vanderbilt II bought it for the Metropolitan Museum of Art, where it is still displayed, having lost none of its popular appeal in the one hundred fifty years since it was painted.

Stewart died in 1876, his widow in 1886. Cornelia Stewart's nephews and nieces (one of whom married Stanford White) inherited large fortunes. The great marble mansion was sold to the Manhattan Club, which stayed there until 1899, when the members found the maintenance of the palace too heavy for their subscriptions. It was demolished after the turn of the century and replaced by a bank.

No one else built a marble house, but building became frenzied in the neighborhood. Between the 1850s and the 1880s, Fifth Avenue between Fourteenth and Forty-second streets became an almost unbroken row of brownstone houses. They were uniform in size, and little effort was made to differentiate them in style. The brownstone was applied over brick or plaster or wood. If the real product was too expensive, so eager were residents to live in "a brownstone" that the front of the house was sometimes plastered to resemble brownstone. The very name of these buildings, "row houses" indicated their monotony. (The term *town house* for these buildings is twentieth-century real-estate flattery.) Some of the owners were very rich indeed and socially well-connected, but you would not know it from the outside of their houses.

The monotonous brownstones may help account for some of the unkind words about New York City from foreign visitors in the Civil War era. When Anthony Trollope published his hefty *North America* in 1861, he was quite sarcastic about Fifth Avenue: "I know no great man, no cele-brated statesman, no philanthropist of peculiar note who has lived on Fifth Avenue," he wrote. "That gentleman on the right made a million of dollars by inventing a shirt-collar; this one on the left electrified the world by a lotion.... Such are the aristocracy of Fifth Avenue." And another Briton, Edward Dicey, who reported the Civil War for the *London Spectator*, remarked, "Fifth Avenue is symmetrical enough; but its semi-detached stone mansions, handsome as they are, have not sufficient height to justify its American name of the Street of Palaces; while its monotony is dreadful...."

The interiors of the brownstones were much more favorably appraised by Europeans: they were warm, they were well furnished, and they had conveniences such as gas lighting, piped-in water, and bathrooms. In the comforts of technology they were far ahead of European dwellings. However, they were overcrowded with furniture, increasingly so after the Civil War, when the overstuffed taste that can best be described as *horror vacui* flourished.

The years between 1868 and 1872 saw a frenzy of construction along and around Fifth Avenue from the streets numbered in the high Twenties to the Forties, one of a long series of real-estate booms that have dotted New York City's history. Most of these houses were not erected by their owners but by speculative builders, who then sold or rented them.

By the 1880s, Fifth Avenue in the Twenties and Thirties was a busy but pleasant mixture of residences, clubs, fine shops, hotels, and restaurants. The Albemarle Hotel was at Twenty-fourth Street, the Victoria at Twenty-seventh, the Holland House at Thirtieth, and the Cambridge at Thirty-third Street. All of them were first-class, dignified, and not "commercial," not catering to business travelers since they were far from the commercial center of the city, which was not easy to reach due to the slowness of travel in Manhattan. Allen Dodworth's famous dancing classes were held in a building on the southeast corner of Fifth Avenue and Twenty-sixth Street. Children of the socially prominent attended these classes; the memoirist Mabel Osgood Wright remembered dancing in the 1870s with a bumptious little boy named Theodore Roosevelt.

The Cosmos Club opened at 98 Fifth Avenue (organized in 1885, the club required members to read Alexander von Humboldt's *Cosmos*). The Blossom Club was at number 129 from 1870 on, the Travellers' at 124 in 1872, and the Lotos, a literary club, about the same time at number 147. The Knickerbocker Club, organized by eighteen dissatisfied members of the Union Club, was at 319 Fifth Avenue at Thirty-second Street. The Calumet Club was at 267 Fifth Avenue and described as "a club for the men whom the limit of membership and the long waiting list keep out of the Union." At Fifth Avenue and Twenty-seventh Street the Reform Club had its own building. It was organized in 1888 "to promote honest, efficient and economical government," a brave but not very promising aim in civically corrupt New York. At 212 Fifth Avenue was the Sorosis Club for women, founded in 1868 for the high-minded goal of "the discussion and dissemination of principles and facts which promise to exert a salutary influence on women and society."

Delmonico's restaurant moved to Twenty-sixth Street in 1876, on a very desirable plot fronting on both Fifth Avenue and Broadway. The food there, which included such specialties as baked Alaska, a heated ice pudding, was sumptuous. This location, one of nine or more occupied by the restaurant during its history, was the scene of the "Swan Dinner," given by a rich German-born banker, Henry Lukemeyer. His guests dined at a table covered with violets and centered with a pond on which floated swans brought from Prospect Park in Brooklyn. The swans had been drugged to keep them quiet, but as the evening wore on, the swans began to come to life, nibbling first at the violets and then at the guests, who huddled in terror until the indignant birds were captured and dispatched back to Brooklyn. Sherry's, Delmonico's principal competitor, opened in 1890 farther north at Fifth Avenue and Thirty-seventh Street. The presence of these two institutions was a sure sign that the neighborhood was becoming fashionable.

"Ladies' Mile," along Broadway from Fourteenth to Twenty-third streets and Sixth Avenue below Twenty-third Street, was the principal shopping area in post–Civil War New York. Nevertheless, along Fifth Avenue were some of the expensive specialty shops favored by the rich, most of them devoted to personal attire. At 305 Fifth Avenue, C. F. Janson sold "rich

The Marble Collegiate Church, founded in 1628, is the oldest Dutch Reformed congregation in North America. In 1854, the church dedicated a new building on the northwest corner of Fifth Avenue and Twenty-ninth Street. The Gothic Revival church features Tiffany stained glass windows. Its school, the Collegiate School, was founded in 1687 and is the oldest in the city.

fur" jackets, capes, and muffs. At F. Booss & Brothers, situated at 290 Fifth Avenue, between Thirtieth and Thirty-first streets, "seal coats [were]a specialty." At 345 Fifth, opposite the Astor houses, was Watkins, a "Ladies' Tailor," and around the corner at 32 West Thirty-second Street was Bergdorf and Goodman, "tailors and dressmakers," which became one of the most famous and long-lasting mercantile names on Fifth

Avenue. Corsets, or "stays," were then universally worn by women, and at 13 West Thirty-third Street they could have the necessaries repaired at the Corset Hospital and the American-Belgium corset laundry.

New shops changed the appearance of Fifth Avenue by breaking the monotonous row of brownstones. In 1903 *Town & Country* hailed the "invasion of commerce" for that reason: "The brown-stone streets are blossoming out, here and there, with odd houses, all designed for business purposes. They break the monotonous line and make that part of the city a place of pleasant contrasts...." The magazine also praised the discreet appearance of the new shops: "They are established in large residences, slightly altered...made very attractive and still with show windows which only contain a hint of buying and selling."

From 1893 to 1929, the great ornament of this section of Fifth Avenue was the Waldorf-Astoria Hotel, during a relatively short life of three decades one of the legendary attractions of New York City. When the hotel was built, it stood proudly at the new center of New York social life; by the time it shut its doors, society had moved uptown and to the east and the neighborhood had become largely commercial. The name itself was a valuable asset, preserved in the second, even grander, present-day Waldorf-Astoria Hotel on Park Avenue at Fiftieth Street.

The first Waldorf-Astoria was much more than a commercial hostelry. It was the favored stopping place of royalty and nobility and diplomats. Official guests of the American government stayed at the Waldorf-Astoria when they visited New York. Financial magnates, as distinct from mere businessmen, favored it for informal meetings: J. P. Morgan might be spotted in its lobby or Men's Cafe, along with Judge Elbert H. Gary, chairman of U.S. Steel, and the raffish speculator John "Bet-a-Million" Gates, who earned his fortune selling barbed wire and his nickname by wagers on practically anything that moved.

The special atmosphere of the Waldorf-Astoria, however, came from its immediate adoption by New York society as its favorite place away from home. Many of the social elect lived in apartments at the hotel, and more entertained there. The Waldorf had the good fortune to open just at the time when it became fashionable to entertain away from home. Until the

Henry J. Hardenbergh, architect of the first Waldorf-Astoria Hotel, built in 1893 on the southwest corner of Fifth Avenue and Thirty-fourth Street (later the site of the Empire State Building), claimed that his design was "German Renaissance" in tribute to the ancestral home of the Astor family. The Waldorf-Astoria received New York's most distinguished foreign guests and entertained New York society for more than three decades.

late nineteenth century, people aware of their social position entertained guests only in their own houses. If you gave a ball, it was in your own ball-room, and certainly all dinners, except public banquets (attended only by men), were given at home. However, as entertainments grew larger and more elaborate and domestic servants scarcer, the rich began to enjoy the luxury of having trained hotel staff assume the burdens of dinner for fifty guests and a ball for five hundred. This change was closely related to the change in women's activities: women were going out more, and it was no longer unusual to see upper-class women giving parties in hired rooms.

Entertaining at the Waldorf-Astoria was socially acceptable partly because the hotel was the property of the Astors, New York's most socially vigilant, not to say dictatorial, family. The Astors were in the hotel business long before they built the Waldorf-Astoria. Since 1836 they had owned the Astor House, a large hotel on Broadway between Vesey and Barclay streets, once the city's finest but in recent years increasingly the resort of traveling salesmen and too far downtown to attract society. It was demolished in 1913, in the course of subway construction under Broadway. The Astors were to build the Knickerbocker on West Forty-second Street in 1906 and the New Netherland on the northeast corner of Fifth Avenue and Fifty-ninth Street in 1893, followed by the jewel of the Astor hotels, the St. Regis, on the southeast corner of Fifth Avenue and Fifty-fifth Street.

Their vast Waldorf-Astoria at Fifth Avenue and Thirty-fourth Street was built as much the result of a family feud as of careful planning. The land beneath it had already been Astor property for sixty years. In 1827, William B. Astor bought a half interest in the twenty-acre John Thompson farm in what was then undeveloped upper Manhattan for $20,500. Included in the purchase was land along Fifth Avenue from Thirty-second to Thirty-fifth streets.

William B. Astor had two sons, John Jacob Astor III and William B., Jr. The brothers, although very different—John Jacob was responsible and serious, William pleasure-loving and carefree—got along well enough, as did their wives. John Jacob was married to Charlotte Augusta Gibbes, a Southerner of prominent family noted for her good nature and her many charities. William was married to the formidable Caroline Webster Schermerhorn (Aunt Lina, to the family), descendant of a rich old New York Dutch family. She was to become the most famous figure in American society, the hostess and social arbiter of the Gilded Age.

The trouble arose in the next generation. John Jacob and Charlotte Augusta had but one child, William Waldorf Astor, whose middle name was that of the German village where the first John Jacob Astor was born.

From his childhood, he considered himself a superior person. Spoiled and difficult, he had a conviction that his merits were insufficiently recognized by his fellow citizens. He regarded his opinions as precious, but despite his pedigree and his wealth, they were not highly regarded or even listened to. He was elected to the New York State Assembly and then the New York State Senate, was appointed ambassador to Italy—political contributions played a role there—and wrote two thunder-and-lightning historical novels with Italian Renaissance themes, yet he remained unsatisfied and widely disliked. Like many people who really have nothing to do, he busied himself with social trivia and made himself unhappy by fancying slights of the most insignificant kind.

After he married Philadelphia aristocrat Mary Dahlgren Paul (called Mamie) in 1878, he insisted that she be referred to simply as Mrs. Astor. He was correct: the convention of the time was that the wife of the eldest male member of a family be referred to that way, following the rule that the higher the rank, the simpler the name. Unfortunately, because he and his wife were absent in Italy during his ambassadorship and because Mrs. William B. Astor's social maneuvering was so effective, the press and society had fallen into the habit of referring to Mrs. William B. Astor as Mrs. Astor. This was wormwood and gall to William Waldorf: Mamie, wife of the senior male of the line, was Mrs. Astor. (The lady herself regarded the matter with the indifference of a Philadelphia aristocrat.) Thereupon began a feud between William Waldorf and his Aunt Lina.

When Waldorf's father died in 1890 and his house on the northwest corner of Fifth Avenue and Thirty-third Street, next door to Mr. and Mrs. William B., became vacant, it occurred to him to build a large hotel on the lot. No more offensive act could be imagined; it was the perfect revenge, to build a large, noisy hotel next door to his aunt's social holy of holies. Waldorf insisted that the hotel be named the Waldorf to remind the American public of his importance, although by the time it was completed he lived in England and saw his hotel only once in his life.

Plans for the hotel were filed with the city on 7 November 1890, and construction of the thirteen-story building took three years. The cost was four million dollars. Architect Henry J. Hardenbergh built it in the German Renaissance style, another bow to the Astor heritage. *King's Handbook,* an indispensable guide to New York at the time, said that it was "abounding in loggias, balconies, gables, groups of chimneys and tiled roofs." The Waldorf immediately surpassed all other hotels in New York, even the great Fifth Avenue. It had 530 rooms, of which 450 were bedrooms, the others being sitting room suites; even more remarkably for the time, it had 350 private bathrooms. Walls and furnishings from the John Jacob Astor residence were thriftily installed in the public dining room. Although the telephone company, which had opened in New York in 1878, had fifteen thousand subscribers, there were no private telephones in the Waldorf until 1902. Guests had to use an elaborate system of bells to summon maids, messengers, hairdressers, waiters, and so on, each of which had a special bell. The call system naturally required an immense staff.

Two floors of the Waldorf were reserved for male guests who were alone. B. C. Forbes, founder of *Forbes* magazine, and Judge Gary lived there for a time. Forbes had a regular poker club with Henry Clay Frick; Herman Freasch, "The Sulphur King"; Herman Sielcken, "The Coffee King"; and other prominent plutocrats among the players. Colonel E. H. R. Green, son and heir of Hetty Green, the investor known unflatteringly as the Witch of Wall Street, lived at the Waldorf for years surrounded by his celebrated stamp collection, his unique collection of uncut gems, and various attractive young women in a sixteen-room suite for which he paid twenty-eight thousand dollars a year. He was believed to have spent one hundred fifty thousand dollars on the suite's decoration.

The general manager was George Boldt, who became a legend for his efficiency and tender care of his guests and for his tyranny over his hundreds of employees. There was a great storm among the male staff when he decreed that no waiter could wear a beard. In an age of masculine facial hair, this rule seemed to strike at the very essence of maledom, but Boldt made it stick: at the Waldorf only the guests wore beards.

On 14 March 1893 the Waldorf opened its doors with a party for the benefit of St. Mary's Free Hospital for Children. Raising funds for charity by charging large sums for tickets to parties was an idea already well established in New York society. The auspices were socially impeccable. Mrs. Richard Irvin, active in innumerable charities (and one of the original "Four Hundred") was the "patroness," and Mrs. William K. Vanderbilt paid for the opening concert by the New York Symphony led by Walter Damrosch. The program included excerpts from *Carmen* and a piece for the cello by Max Bruch; it concluded grandly with the prelude to *Die Meistersinger Von Nürnberg.*

The Waldorf Hotel was a smashing success with the public and very profitable for the Astor interests. It succeeded also in achieving William Waldorf Astor's unpublicized purpose: it drove his Aunt Lina from Thirty-fourth Street. Annoyed by a bustling hotel next door, she closed her house and commissioned Richard Morris Hunt to build her a larger and in every way more splendid residence far up Fifth Avenue at Sixty-fifth Street. Where 350 Fifth Avenue had stood rose another hotel, the Astoria, built by her son, John Jacob Astor IV. He first thought to call his hotel the Schermerhorn after his mother's family, but decided on the Astoria to recall the first John Jacob Astor's fur-trading settlement on the west coast.

The Astoria had a Fifth Avenue frontage, but its length was along West Thirty-fourth Street. The two hotels were not the same height, the Astoria being five stories taller, but were connected and effectively one building. Provision was made so that the hotels could be divided at any time, apparently a nod to the uneasy relations between the two branches of the family. The architect again was Henry J. Hardenbergh, the style again German Renaissance.

The combined Waldorf-Astoria opened with a charity concert on 1 November 1897. The double hotel was the largest in the world with 1,000 rooms and 765 private baths. The wide hall that connected the two buildings quickly became a favorite strolling—and strutting—place for New York society; wags called the hall Peacock Alley. The hotel had no objection, and soon the nickname was so recognizable that it was a topical reference in plays; one comedy, *The Earl of Pawtucket*, even had a scene laid in Peacock Alley. The name was carried over to the new Waldorf-Astoria, when it was built in 1931, and is used today.

In 1900 *Harper's Bazaar* declared that the Waldorf-Astoria was "the fashion of New York and the Mecca of visitors…here is the chosen gathering place of New York society, which comes here to see and to be observed…." The management, well aware of the value of publicity, had imposing statistics available for reporters: in one day, 19,867 people passed through the thirteen doors of the building; there were more than 360,000 guests during a year and 412,000 nonresident guests.

The hotel's food became famous under the guidance of Oscar Michel Tschirky, a Swiss who became known worldwide as Oscar of the Waldorf. He carefully selected food to suit the prevailing tastes of the rich, which they consumed in quantities that are unimaginable today. Game birds, for example, were served in amazing quantities; the hotel's kitchens often used 300 partridges a day. Late in the evening, after the theater, lobster Newburg was the dish most in demand; some nights the hotel served a thousand portions. On New Year's Eve, the hotel had four or five thousand guests who ate 750 chickens, 1,000 pounds of lobster, 20 barrels of oysters, 500 quail, and 250 wild ducks.

A year after the hotel opened, Charles Steinway, an heir to the piano-manufacturing fortune, gave a dinner to thirty-one guests (including, unusually, ladies) with a much admired menu consisting of

DEVILED EGGS
OYSTERS
GREEN TURTLE SOUP
MOUSSE OF BASS SHAPED AS TURBANS AND SERVED WITH CUCUMBERS
BREAST OF CHICKEN WITH MADEIRA SAUCE
CRABS WITH MUSHROOMS
BRAISED SADDLE OF LAMB WITH HAM, POTATOES AND FRENCH PEAS
SHERBERT
TERRAPIN
CANVASBACK DUCK WITH CURRENT JELLY
CELERY SALAD WITH MAYONNAISE
ICE CREAM WITH CAKES AND FRUIT
COFFEE
CHABLIS, BERNKASTELER DOKTOR, RAUENTHALER BERG, MEDOC,
AND POMMERY WINES, AND APOLLINARIS WATER

According to accounts, the thirty-one guests consumed 137 quarts of wine and mineral water and 32 bottles of liqueurs and brandy!

Around 1900 the Waldorf-Astoria opened a room for the service of afternoon tea called the Palm Court, decorated with a thicket of the palm trees in tubs so beloved by the era. Entertainment was furnished by costumed Tyroleans who sang, danced, and yodeled during the tea hour. After dinner an orchestra played in the lobby while waiters in Turkish dress served coffee.

Ladies had always entered hotels by the "ladies' entrance" to avoid the attention of male loungers around the front door who might make impertinent remarks, but the Waldorf-Astoria made its lobby so attractive that ladies came in through the front door. In 1907, George Boldt daringly posted a notice that read "Ladies without escorts will be served in the restaurants at any hour." The time was the innovation: women were already lunching in restaurants without male escorts, but dining without them was unthinkable. Boldt's move upset the city's moral guardians and was widely criticized, but worse, from their point of view, was to follow: in 1911 the Corporation Council of New York ruled that women could smoke in the dining rooms of hotels. For a long time there were few women who dared use this "privilege"; most did not smoke in public until the general relaxing of the old rules that followed World War I.

When the Waldorf opened, the Men's Cafe had no bar, probably to set it apart from New York's ubiquitous saloons; you had to sit at a table to drink, a risky change since leaning on the bar was regarded as a special badge of masculinity. It caught on, however, like most of the Waldorf's changes, a certain indication of the hotel's social authority, and the Men's Cafe was soon the gathering place of financiers—and speculators, too. It was a good place to raise capital: a meeting there between tycoons resulted, in 1901, in the creation of the U.S. Steel Corporation, at the time the biggest company in the world.

The bars in the Waldorf-Astoria were noted for their mixed drinks. Cocktails became popular in America during the early nineteenth century; nearly every foreign visitor from Charles Dickens onward, amazed by the fiery concoctions that Americans drank at all hours, mentioned cocktails in their accounts of the United States. In the early twentieth century before Prohibition the art of cocktail mixing became a veritable science. The Waldorf-Astoria's bartenders were constantly dreaming up new combinations, many of them nearly lethal by today's standards, and giving them names to remind drinkers of the hotel: there was the Waldorf

Gloom Lifter (Irish whisky, Martell brandy, an egg white, raspberry syrup, grenadine, sugar, and ice), the Peacock Alley (rum, maple syrup, lime juice, and ice), and the Waldorf Fizz (gin, orange juice, lemon juice, an egg, sugar, and ice). All these were shaken cocktails, and the sight of a row of bartenders each with his shaker must have been a comforting sight to customers on a drizzly day in New York. A favorite after-dinner drink was the Pousse-Cafe Waldorf: into a sherry glass were carefully poured, in the following precise order, raspberry syrup, anisette, parfait d'amour, creme Yvette, yellow Chartreuse, green Chartreuse, and Cordon bleu brandy.

The Waldorf-Astoria catered not only to travelers and resident guests; it had a large and profitable business in renting rooms—there were forty public rooms available—for special events and catering them. In a typical year before World War I there were 1,714 banquets and other entertainments given in the hotel, 175 concerts, lectures and plays, and 427 meetings.

The best-known concerts were George Bagby's "Musical Mornings," so well attended by prominent ladies that the historian Dixon Wecter referred to the impresario as "the Orpheus of Society." A contemporary described him as a "little man with waxed mustaches who inspires such faith in his lady patrons that they never ask what his program will be." During the winter season he presented weekly concerts of solid classical music performed by the best-known professionals. The morning concerts were followed by a "breakfast" in the Grand Ballroom of the hotel.

The air of elegant bustle around the Waldorf-Astoria was well caught by Willa Cather in her 1905 short story "Paul's Case: A Study in Temperament":

> There were a score of cabs about the entrance of his hotel, and his driver had to wait. Boys in livery were running in and out of the awning stretched across the sidewalk, up and down the red velvet carpet laid from the door to the street. Above, about, within it all was the rumble and roar, the hurry and toss of thousands of human beings as hot for pleasure as himself, and on every side of him towered the glaring affirmation of the omnipotence of wealth.

Although the interior of the Waldorf-Astoria was an attempt at Italian Renaissance and Empire decor, the effect was Edwardian deluxe, the style of the Paris Ritz and other grand international hotels, which offered a new combination of stateliness and ease. The Waldorf-Astoria was noted for its army of staff, including numerous bellmen required to stand at attention with arms crossed, as pictured here.

An important early event was the first automobile parade held in New York, which began at the Waldorf-Astoria on 4 November 1899 and proceeded up Fifth Avenue to the foot of Central Park at Fifty-ninth Street; that was as far as the automobiles were allowed to go because motorcars were still prohibited in the park. Two years later, the first automobile show in America was held at Madison Square Garden; the machines were shown in motion on a wooden track.

Automobiles caught on more quickly than many other inventions. Taxicabs were first introduced onto Fifth Avenue in 1907. By 1911 *Town & Country* magazine wrote in an editorial on the traffic situation that "a glance up or down Fifth Avenue these days makes it very evident that the motor reigns supreme. Nearly everything on wheels is propelled by gasoline or electricity. Instead of the dreary stages, drawn by tired horses, presumably in the last agonies of starvation…there are huge top-heavy monsters…."

Privately owned motorcars were becoming very popular. At first they were treated as carriages: "The chauffeur and footman have picturesque liveries," *Town & Country* wrote, "and the many limousines and landaulettes and other varieties of cars which now crowd the Avenue, are works of art."

Another hotel in the neighborhood was Holland House, on the southwest corner of Thirtieth Street. Much smaller than the Waldorf-Astoria, it was equally elegant. The management was especially proud of an electric indicator called the Herzog Teleseme in each room, a dial listing one hundred forty different articles (newspapers, bottles of wine, food, or a servant) that could be ordered directly from the front desk. The guest had merely to move a pointer and push the proper button. The English textile firm of Wilton's supplied the carpets, the silverware was commissioned from Gorham, the china was Royal Worcester, and the table linen for the hotel was woven in Scotland.

On the southwest corner of Fifth and Thirty-third Street, facing the Waldorf, was the Hotel Cambridge, largely occupied by families who used it as their winter home in the city. On the American plan with all meals supplied, it charged five dollars per day and up. The management boasted that the hotel "was far enough away from Broadway to avoid all its commotions, and yet close enough to enjoy its conveniences."

Benjamin Altman was a second-generation dry-goods merchant whose family store was on Sixth Avenue at West Nineteenth Street, in the heart of a long-established shopping district. Trade in that old retail neighborhood was weakening as its customers moved farther uptown. In the 1890s Altman began to acquire property for a new and greatly expanded department store east and diagonally across Fifth Avenue from the new Waldorf-Astoria. The neighborhood was still largely residential, and the residents were exactly the type he wanted to reach. Construction began in 1906. By that time, Altman had purchased all the Fifth Avenue frontage except the corner at East Thirty-fourth Street, which was occupied by M. Knoedler & Co., an art gallery that held out for nearly a decade before selling and allowing Altman to complete his Fifth Avenue facade in 1914. Roland Knoedler, the owner, moved uptown to an English-style townhouse at 556 Fifth Avenue, near Forty-seventh Street, where the firm remained until 1925, when it moved to East Fifty-seventh Street, then and for many years the center of the art trade in New York.

The architects of the B. Altman store were the aristocratic firm of Trowbridge & Livingston, and they produced for him one of the most majestic emporiums ever constructed, a dignified building, eight stories high on Fifth Avenue and twelve stories on Madison, that looked more like a financial institution than a department store. Trowbridge & Livingston were responsible for other stately buildings in New York, including J. P. Morgan & Company's offices on Wall Street. The restraint exercised in the Altman store was partly intended to placate nearby residents, who were opposed to all stores on Fifth Avenue, even one modeled on an Italian Renaissance palace like Altman's. The owner and the architects were very respectful of these sensibilities; the name of the store did not even appear on the facade for decades.

From the first, Altman's catered to an upper-class clientele. It had an air of leisurely shopping in pleasant surroundings, with open spaces and highly polished wood floors. Chauffeurs could park motorcars on East Thirty-fifth Street, and there was a bell system by which they could be summoned to the front door when the lady had completed her shopping. Altman's opened at a time when women of the middle and upper classes were transforming shopping into a leisure activity as well as a search for necessities. Few, if any, other retail establishments so endeared themselves to the public as Altman's, with its restaurants, lounges, tearooms, tasteful gift-wrapping, and elaborate window displays at holidays. Increasingly outmoded and subject to several changes of ownership, it was mourned, nevertheless, when it finally went out of business in 1989. The noble building remained to take on new life as the B. Altman Advanced Learning Superblock, housing the science, industry, and business branch of the New York Public Library, Oxford University Press, and the Graduate Center of the City University of New York.

In 1928 the two-acre plot on the southwest corner of Fifth Avenue and Thirty-fourth Street—formerly the John Thompson farm in 1799;

William B. Astor's land in 1827; the home of his sons, William B., Jr., and John Jacob, in 1856; and the Waldorf-Astoria Hotel in the 1890s— became the site of the Empire State Building. The hotel was showing its age: society had moved on, uptown as usual, to the St. Regis and the hotels around the Grand Army Plaza, for its obligations and festivities, and both the architecture and the entertainment of the Waldorf had begun to seem dated. A new Waldorf-Astoria was planned for Park Avenue significantly farther uptown, between East Forty-ninth and Fiftieth streets.

In a burst of 1920s optimism a consortium led by John J. Raskob, head of the General Motors Corporation, and Pierre S. du Pont bought the site from the Astor family for about twenty million dollars. The titular head of the corporation formed to erect a building was Alfred E. Smith, former

In the 1920s, the intersection of Fifth Avenue and Thirty-fourth Street was the most popular place on the avenue to shop. At the right is the stately B. Altman store; three blocks north was the Tiffany store. The flagpoles at left are those of the Waldorf-Astoria Hotel. The installation in 1919 of the first traffic tower, like the one in the foreground, marked the advent of a primitive system of traffic lights in the city.

governor of New York State (the "Empire State"). Shreve, Lamb, and Harmon were the architects. They produced a handsome, up-to-the-minute building in the art deco style. At 1,250 feet, it was the tallest building in the world, taller by 200 feet than the Chrysler Building on East Forty-second Street. Of the 102 stories, 85 were for offices, shops, and an observation deck. Sixteen stories were a "mooring mast" for the dirigibles which the corporation hoped would tie up. They did not, because no one could ever devise a safe way to get the passengers down from the dirigible into the building.

All work records for the construction of such a mammoth edifice were broken: the Waldorf-Astoria was demolished in October 1929 (an ominous date, for the Great Depression began that month), the Empire State's first columns were laid in April 1930, and the building was dedicated on 1 May 1931. The work force sometimes numbered 3,500, and in one ten-day period, fourteen stories were added.

As a symbol, the building gave hope to New Yorkers during the Depression. As a business venture, it was not so successful: fifteen years passed before it was fully rented. The location, which had seemed so prime in 1929, was not, as it turned out, the best. The financial industry remained stubbornly concentrated on the lower end of the island, where it had been since Dutch days, and for other businesses, Rockefeller Center, emerging at exactly the same time, offered a more elegant location farther uptown.

Great buildings, from the Tower of London to the Pentagon, create their own folklore. The Empire State Building is richer than most. The famous final scene of the 1933 motion picture *King Kong*, showing the giant ape climbing the building while fighting off airborne attackers, became so much an American memory that its fiftieth anniversary was celebrated in state by hanging a 3,000-pound inflatable Kong from the upper floors of the building. The Empire State's statistics endear it to visitors: seven miles of elevator shafts, 6,500 windows, 1,860 steps from the ground floor to the 102d floor.

Despite its original lack of success, despite the fact that in the 1970s the World Trade Center surpassed it in height, despite many changes of

During the nineteenth century, art dealers, many of them European, opened ground floor galleries, and sometimes galleries occupying entire buildings. When Benjamin Altman was planning to open his department store on the block bounded by Thirty-fourth and Thirty-fifth streets and Fifth and Madison Avenues, he was impeded by art dealer Roland Knoedler, who refused to surrender his gallery, M. Knoedler & Co., on the northeast corner of Fifth Avenue and Thirty-fourth Street. Altman was forced to build around the building occupied by Knoedler's gallery, but later obtained the site and completed his store.

ownership, lawsuits, and charges of neglecting the structure, the Empire State Building remains the most recognizable and therefore the most powerful symbol of the city. It is to New York what the Eiffel Tower is to Paris. The lasting affection of the public for the building, and their interest in it, has never been equaled by the Chrysler Building, Rockefeller Center, or the twin towers of the World Trade Center. As early as 1937,

On 16 December 1930, the photographer Robert A. Knudtsen stood on the forty-second floor of an office building on Eighth Avenue to take this photograph of the uncompleted Empire State Building at Fifth Avenue and Thirty-fourth Street. Worldwide enthusiasm for dirigible flight prompted the construction of a mast to be used as a mooring; however, it was only used once.

when thirty floors were said to be vacant and the lights in empty suites were being turned on to make the building look fully rented, Hurlbert Footner spoke for many when he wrote, "It is one of the great sights of earth; a panorama of power and beauty and terror such as the world never offered before. It gives a quite ordinary man some godlike moments."

4

Mercantile Renaissance

Thirty-fourth Street to Forty-second Street

•

The western edge of the neighborhood, long called Murray Hill after a Quaker family who lived there in colonial times, lay along Fifth Avenue between Thirty-fourth and Forty-second streets. After the Civil War, as development proceeded up Fifth Avenue, these eight blocks became a desirable residential neighborhood. Members of the Astor family, who owned much of the real estate, led the way. The building of houses by William and John Jacob Astor at Thirty-fourth Street and Fifth Avenue and by various of their kin on the avenue and the surrounding side streets helped make the area socially acceptable (and added to the ever-increasing Astor fortune).

Although the difference in elevation from lower Fifth Avenue is almost imperceptible today due to grading and leveling of the streets, Murray Hill seemed to nineteenth-century New Yorkers to be salubrious high ground. It was, in fact, higher than any other residential neighborhood in New York built by that time. People were much concerned about elevation, which, even though it might be only a few feet, they were convinced provided "pure air." "Higher and drier" was the slogan when considering a site for your house. In a time of deadly fevers brought on by poor drainage that killed thousands of New Yorkers each year, the expression had real meaning.

The major attraction of the neighborhood from 1842 on was the Croton Reservoir at Fifth Avenue and Forty-second Street. The history of several great spaces along Fifth Avenue can ultimately be traced to their use as a potter's field: Washington Square, Madison Square, and the site of the reservoir, later of the New York Public Library and Bryant Park. For a short time, from 1822 to 1825, the square block bounded by Fortieth and Forty-second streets and by Fifth and Sixth avenues was a burial ground for paupers, replacing the one closed at Washington Square.

A decade later, construction began on a reservoir to store water brought from the Croton Dam in Putnam County. It was the termination of a forty-two-mile long aqueduct that began at the Croton Dam, traveled the High Bridge over the Harlem River, emptied into a lake called the North Reservoir between Seventy-ninth and Eighty-sixth streets in what became Central Park, and ended in an enormous structure on Fifth Avenue and Forty-second Street. From the reservoir clean water was piped all over the city, which had been depending for two centuries on increasingly polluted wells. Building the Croton Aqueduct was one of the great feats of nineteenth-century American engineering, and the importance of the clean water it brought to New York City can hardly be exaggerated. A plentiful supply was immediately available for sewage and street cleaning. The appearance of New York City and the health of its citizens, at least of its middle-class citizens, were noticeably bettered; in many ways the improvement enabled New York to become a great city. Alas, the benefits did not penetrate the worst slums, where the inhabitants could not afford even the reasonable charges for Croton water. They spread festeringly for generations to come.

The four-acre reservoir was divided into two deep basins. The architecture was monumental; strangely, the reservoir resembled an Egyptian temple, with walls forty-one and a half feet high and wide enough at top for promenading. Splendid views of the city, still without tall buildings, could be had, or "taken" as the expression then was, from the top.

At sunrise on the Fourth of July, 1842, the gigantic Croton Reservoir at Fifth Avenue and Forty-second Street, which was to supply the city for the first time with a reliable source of clean water, officially opened. A month later, the water began to flow to buildings that had been supplied with pipes and fittings. The reservoir, planted with trees and flowers along its walls, became a favorite excursion spot, affording fresh air and views of the low-rise city. The New York Public Library now occupies the site.

The reservoir fascinated New Yorkers; a stroll up Fifth Avenue ending at the reservoir was a favorite after-church amusement for New Yorkers on Sundays. Edgar Allan Poe, editing *The Broadway Journal*, recommended the excursion heartily: "When you visit Gotham, you should ride out the Fifth Avenue, or as far as the distributing reservoir....The prospect from the walk around the reservoir is particularly beautiful. You can see from this elevation, the north reservoir at Yorkville, the whole city to the Battery, with a large portion of the harbor, and long reaches of the Hudson and East rivers."

Across from the reservoir on the southeast corner of Fifth Avenue and Fortieth Street was a food stand, Croton Cottage, where strollers refreshed themselves with ice cream (then a novelty) after a promenade around the reservoir. The cottage was burned down in the "draft riots" in 1863 and the lot bought by William H. Vanderbilt, who built a brownstone house there, modest by the later standards of Vanderbilt houses on Fifth Avenue, and gave it to his son Frederick. The site later became the Arnold Constable department store and, eventually, a branch of the New York Public Library.

On the northwest corner of Fifth Avenue and Thirty-seventh Street from 1845 to 1857 a Gothic-style house, often called a villa because it stood in its own gardens, ornamented the neighborhood. It was one of the very few buildings in a neighborhood still largely rural; Mrs. Waddell is said to have waited under a nearby apple tree while her husband, William Coventry H. Waddell, negotiated for the property. Their house was designed by Alexander Jackson Davis, responsible also for the New York University buildings at Washington Square. The Waddell house was called by Davis on his plans "a suburban Gothic Villa, Murray Hill, N. Y. City." The bucolic title indicates how distant New Yorkers thought Murray Hill was from the city.

The Waddell villa was turreted and castellated and had an oriel window and was surrounded by a decorative iron fence into which had been wrought the name "W. Coventry Waddell." A glassed-in two-story addition was marked on the plan "painting gallery." The villa was demolished in 1857, and the following year the Brick Presbyterian Church, designed by Leopold Eidlitz and Griffith Thomas, was built on the site. Unexpectedly, it looked like a small Roman temple. The church, founded in 1767 near City Hall Park, had sold its downtown property as had so many old churches. The cost of the new edifice, including land, was $288,000, making it the most expensive building constructed in the city to that time. It remained on the site until 1937.

Davis was also the architect of a group of castellated Gothic houses, eleven in all, built in 1855 on the east side of Fifth Avenue between Forty-first and Forty-second streets, opposite the reservoir, and numbered 487–91 Fifth Avenue. They were terrace housing in the English manner, townhouses in a row with common walls. The terrace was quickly nicknamed the "House of Mansions." The builder, George Higgins, thought

Across Fifth Avenue from the Croton Reservoir, eleven connected and castellated dwellings called the "House of Mansions" were built in 1855. The Gothic-style houses failed to sell because well-to-do New Yorkers preferred to live considerably farther downtown. The little fortresses were then combined into one building to house the Rutgers Female Institute (Rutgers Female College after 1867) until the houses were demolished in 1883.

5TH AVE. LOOKING SOUTH
FROM 42 ND ST. - 1880.-

he could sell the expensive houses to families from downtown seeking the pure air of Murray Hill. He was ahead of his time; in mid-century, few prosperous people wanted to live so far uptown with public transportation so meager and slow. As homes, the houses were not a success and almost immediately were sold to the Rutgers Female Institute, the first institution in the city for the higher education of women, which remained at the address until 1883.

Fifth Avenue would hardly seem the place for reclusiveness, but the avenue has had its share of resident hermits. At number 442, the northwest corner of Thirty-ninth Street, the strange Wendel family maintained a secluded existence for more than eighty years. Their plain four-story house was built about 1850, one of the earliest "uptown" houses on Fifth Avenue. A vacant lot next door was used by them as a dog run. Generations of New Yorkers were fascinated by the Wendel house, visitors too; when sightseeing buses began to travel the avenue, guides loved to point out the "House of Mystery."

John Gottlieb Wendel, head of the German-American family until his death in 1914, was one of New York City's richest and toughest landlords. Noted for his frugality, not to say stinginess, he refused to have steam heat or electricity in the house, used the single old-fashioned zinc bathtub all his life, and never redecorated the threadbare and gloomy dwelling. He raised chickens in the backyard of number 442 to save on meat bills and had the household laundry hung out to dry on the vacant lot, horrifying members of the Union League Club directly across Fifth Avenue. He invariably wore shoes that were sort of elevated galoshes, made for him only, since he was convinced that all diseases invaded the body through the feet touching the ground.

Wendel was a domestic tyrant who refused to allow any of his seven sisters to marry and insisted they dress in the fashions of his Civil War youth. One escaped by eloping—at the age of sixty-one—but the others lived together in the house on Fifth Avenue until 1931, when the last one, Etta Virginia von Echtzel Wendel, died, leaving real estate appraised at thirty-six million dollars scattered all over the city, including such choice parcels as the family home, a dog run, the corners of Broadway and West Thirty-ninth and Broadway and West Fiftieth, and 517 Seventh Avenue.

Etta Wendel's main occupation during her long, secluded life was grooming and exercising her Maltese dog Toby on the vacant Fifth Avenue lot. The name never changed, but of course the dogs were different, a line of seventeen in all. The current Toby always had a place set for him at the dining table and dined alone with Miss Etta. When Toby died, probably of a surfeit of rich food, he was buried in a vault behind the house. The lot where he was exercised was valued at more than a million dollars at Miss Etta's death in the midst of the Great Depression.

Miss Etta, heiress to all her childless predeceased siblings, took no interest in her vast assets and was probably incapable, after no education and a lifetime of isolation, of understanding even the simplest business. Her will, drawn by the decrepit family lawyer, was vague and mentioned no relatives, only a long list of charities, such as the Christian missions in China, of which she could have had little knowledge. Its probate was quickly disputed. Two thousand three hundred and three claimants, most of them doubtful and many bogus, appeared before the New York City Surrogate's Court asserting relationship to Miss Wendel and seeking a share of her fortune. Years of litigation between the estate, the claimants, and the charities named in the will followed, costing millions in legal fees before the estate was settled to the benefit of a few very distant cousins, the charities, and the lawyers.

Although its residents were unusually eccentric, the Wendel house itself was typical of Fifth Avenue architecture. Between 1850 and 1880, brownstones lined the avenue between Washington Square and Fifty-ninth Street; as early as 1860 most of the 340 houses on the avenue were brownstone row houses on standard New York City lots—a 25-foot frontage on the avenue by a 100-foot depth—and were four or five stories in height with a basement and a below-street-front area used as an entry by the servants and tradesmen. A flight of steps with balustrades over that area led to a landing and the front door.

The front steps, or "stoop," were a faint reminder of the Dutch heritage of New York; the word itself is Dutch. In other neighborhoods, but not on Fifth Avenue, these stoops were favored places for New Yorkers to take the air during the city's sweltering summers. "This is an old Knickerbocker custom," wrote Lady Hardy, a British visitor in 1889, "which still obtains everywhere except on the sacred Fifth Avenue, which confines itself strictly within doors, shrined from the vulgar gaze; perhaps the nouveau riche element (being largely represented) is afraid of compromising its dignity by following old-fashioned customs." What the lofty visitor did not realize was that most residents of Fifth Avenue spent the summer out of town at their own summer places or at resorts. If you were obliged for some reason, usually economy, to spend the summer unfashionably in town, you hardly emphasized the fact by sitting on your stoop. Instead, you remained behind drawn shades and had the servants turn away all would-be callers.

Brownstone, in most commentators' eyes, was actually more chocolate than brown in color. Edith Wharton, inclined to sarcasm about her home-town, said that during her childhood "New York looked as though it had been dipped in cold chocolate sauce," and a French visitor said the color was "chocolate au lait." Brownstone was a reddish brown sandstone quarried in New Jersey and cut into sheets with steam machinery. Weathering turned it to chocolate. Unbroken rows of brownstone fronts were extremely monotonous. As early as 1844, Edgar Allan Poe had written, "In some thirty years…the whole island will be densely desecrated by buildings of brick, with portentous facades of brown-stone…." Forty years later, James D. McCabe, a keen observer of the city, wrote, "The principal material used in the construction of the buildings on the avenue is brown stone. This gives to the street a sombre look…. In spite of the general uniformity of the street, however, it is a grand sight upon which the eye rests from any point of view." The only relief to the eye was furnished by gaily colored awnings on each window during the summer and tiled flower boxes full of flowers in season. One commentator wrote lyrically, "Fifth Avenue is exceptionally noticeable for this lavish display of flowers on the window ledges, that seem to be literally blossoming out of the brown stone a little distance away."

Aesthetics aside, the brownstone was a symbol of success to most upper middle-class New Yorkers. In the 1890s *Life* magazine published a joke that ran thus:

> "Will you share my lot, Penelope?"
> "Yes, if there is a brownstone front on it."

One of the peculiarities of the rows of brownstone was that their uniform fronts masked the difference between the rich and the merely well-to-do, producing an unwelcome equality. It was therefore important that the indoor fittings indicate the standing of the residents.

The interiors of brownstones, confined by the twenty-five-foot width, were cramped. A staircase rose from the entrance hall. On the first floor, in a row, were usually a library, a parlor, and a dining room that looked out over the tiny backyard and caught at least a little sunlight in the morning. In his 1893 novel *Katharine Lauderdale*, F. Marion Crawford described such a house:

> In accordance with the customs of the times in which it had
> been built, the ground floor contained three good-sized rooms,
> known in all such houses as the library, the drawing-room or

"parlor" and the dining room, which was at the back and had windows upon the yard. The drawing room, being under the middle of the house, had no windows at all, and was therefore really available only in the evening.

Many dining rooms had originally been in the basement; by the 1880s this was regarded as unhealthy, and the dining room moved upstairs. The parlor and dining room could be thrown together for a party, but the space was not generous. The family bedrooms were on the second and third floors; the fourth floor was usually quarters for staff, of which there would be usually three or four "sleeping in" (these overcrowded and overfurnished houses required a lot of service). The kitchen, the hot-air furnace, and service rooms were in the basement.

In her novel *The Anglomaniacs* Mrs. Burton Harrison describes the modest house of a well-connected literary couple living on a side street just off Fifth Avenue and its inconveniences: "The first floor of the pleasant little home was given up to a narrow passage-way, where on opening the front door the maidservant had to remain caged behind it to allow the entrance of the guest...." The drawing room measured sixteen by twenty feet. The dining room was in the rear of the first floor, so crowded that it required "enforced compression of the maid when circling a table where eight might chance to sit."

The crowded effect was emphasized by the interior decoration fashionable in the second half of the nineteenth century. The structure of the house imposed many limitations. Charles Hanson Towne, no admirer of brownstones, said, "It was the hardest thing in the world to furnish one of those long, lean, dreary drawing rooms, or 'parlors' to break up the monotony of them." Furnishings were eclectic and showy: rosewood furniture remorselessly carved and pierced; numerous mirrors with calling cards and invitations stuck into their frames so that a visitor could see at a glance how socially successful the family was; paintings and framed engravings almost touching each other on the walls and, when wall space ran out, standing on easels scattered about the rooms; statuary perched at angles on perilously tiny pedestals; mantelpieces draped with silk or satin "runners" with a clock in the center and a vase at each end; small tables covered with china, framed photographs, and souvenirs of travel; and fabrics draped artfully but aimlessly over almost every piece of furniture. Therese Yelverton, a British visitor, wrote patronizingly that the "object seems to be so to furnish the house that it may resemble, as nearly as possible, a royal residence. But every article is painted and varnished to look like what it is not." It was the era of "revival" styles, Elizabethan revival or Renaissance revival, for example, in which old period furniture was loosely interpreted for contemporary use, which generally meant making it more ornamented.

By the 1870s the era of "Persian" rugs had arrived (any Near Eastern rug was called Persian). In colonial times they had been imported, but at such great expense that they were too good to walk on and were commonly draped over tables. In the nineteenth century they became much less expensive and in upper middle-class households were laid down over "fitted" (wall-to-wall) carpets. Large animal skins, of a polar bear or leopard for instance, were popular as scatter rugs. Horsehair, slippery to sit on and of a depressing black, had long been the fabric of choice for parlor furniture, but was displaced later in the century by colorful plush, softer and showier. Windows were blanketed with fabrics in dense arrangements. As the New York historian Henry Collins Brown wrote, "houses had a dim religious light and massive layers of curtains." This thick drapery was partly to keep out dust (and New York streets were very dusty in those days) and partly for a more subtle reason: seclusion reinforced the popular concept of the home as the sanctuary of family life.

As the nineteenth century progressed, first floor rooms and halls increasingly blossomed with flowers, rubber plants, potted palms, and other flora. "Botanizing" had become a fashionable pursuit for women; large sums were expended on rare plants. Excess was not frowned on, and some ladies' parlors were junglelike. It became the fashion, for example, to trail vines over paintings and mirrors. Bay windows were transformed into little conservatories by filling them with plants. Those who could afford it and had the space built a true conservatory onto the back of the house. That room was particularly the resort of young people, who "sat out" dances there or flirted while ostensibly admiring the plants. A profusion of greenery was thought conducive to romance; in innumerable novels couples "came to an understanding" and engagements were arranged in conservatories. Plants were the province of the ladies of the house: the watering and, alas, dusting needed in dirty New York, were not done by the maids; ladies reserved these duties to themselves and performed them with dainty gilded watering cans and dusters of high-bred feathers.

Even the numerous critical visitors from abroad admitted that the brownstones were comfortable. Edward Dicey, who published *Six Months in the Federal States* in 1863, wrote, "All the domestic arrangements (to use a fine word for gas, hot water, and other comforts) are wonderfully perfect. Everything, even more than in England, seems adapted for a home life…." "Other comforts" was undoubtedly a delicate reference to sanitation, in which New York was unquestionably far in advance of Britain. Fifth Avenue brownstones usually had full bathrooms. Porcelain bathtubs with taps had replaced the tin tubs that had to be filled and emptied with buckets, a great improvement; tin was difficult to keep clean, and water pouring on tin made an intolerable noise. The houses were, to use a word increasingly popular as the century wore on, "cosy."

Some of these houses were equipped with up-to-date inventions. The first telephones were connected in New York in 1878. Americans have generally been enthralled by new devices, but the telephone did not make particularly rapid progress. Twenty years later, in 1897, the New York telephone company still had only fifteen thousand subscribers. The subscription rate was ten dollars per month. Calls could be placed to a distance of thirty miles.

The subscribers, uncharacteristically timid for New Yorkers, were uneasy with the telephone; it took some time for the etiquette of its use to evolve. You had to speak to an operator, who in the early days was generally male; was it proper for a woman to speak to a strange male? Husbands often placed the calls. Generally, it was determined that the telephone was mainly for use in ordering goods and speaking to shopkeepers; for a long time telephones were kept in the kitchen, handy for the cook. They finally migrated upstairs, where they were often installed in little closet-like rooms off hallways or under the stairs. In the circumstances, long chats over the telephone were quite impossible.

By the 1880s, New Yorkers got uptown to the brownstones by elevated railroad: the Sixth Avenue elevated line began running in 1877, the Third Avenue in 1878, and the Second and Ninth Avenue lines in 1880. There was none on Fifth Avenue, another sign that Fifth was regarded as a boulevard and too elegant for the ugly columns of the elevated and its noisy, spark-spewing trains.

Uptown trains ran on one side of the street, downtown trains on the other, each about thirty feet in the air, their rails supported by iron columns. The trains ran from 5:30 A.M. until midnight, and the service was astoundingly frequent: the Sixth Avenue line alone ran 840 trains a day; during rush hours 70 trains passed per hour. Traffic was immense: small wonder that the lines enriched the companies that built them and were the foundations of great American fortunes like William C. Whitney's and Thomas Fortune Ryan's. The fare was less at rush hours—five cents—than at "off hours," when it was ten cents.

The elevated did not put the street horsecars out of business; there was a line of cars running on iron rails on nearly every avenue except Fifth and on many cross streets. The Fifth Avenue Transportation Company was established in 1885, using horse-drawn omnibuses until 1907, when they were superseded by motor buses.

There were still stagecoaches on Fifth Avenue, but it was considered more dignified to travel by horsecar or the elevated because you were not so jammed up against other passengers. Carriages were available to the public for hire, but they were expensive, costing around a dollar an hour. The fare had to be agreed upon before the trip, or it could become a source of embarrassing controversy in the street. Walter G. Marshall, a British visitor, writing in 1879, cautioned other tourists, "there must be an understanding between yourself and the driver before starting, else there may be a 'scene.'" Maintaining a private carriage was very expensive, like having a limousine and driver today.

Fifth Avenue, like the other principal streets in New York, was disfigured with telephone and telegraph poles. By 1880 it was calculated that there were nine or ten thousand poles on the streets of New York. Charles Hanson Towne remembered "tall telegraph poles and wires stretching interminably over the sidewalks. A more ugly excrescence upon a city's face it would be hard to imagine…." The wires were ideal for birds, especially the ubiquitous English sparrow, to perch on, and at one time birds clustered in such numbers that the city was driven to pass an ordinance making it a misdemeanor to feed them.

The wires of American District Telegraph and other companies connected businesses and homes to a central telegraph office that also supplied burglar and fire alarms. Private homes had a button to summon messengers, who not only picked up and delivered telegrams but also delivered packages and flowers. Messenger boys could be hired as chaperones for unescorted ladies going to the theater. "The neatest boy in the office with the cleanest nose, was delegated as impromptu knight-errant," wrote Henry Collins Brown in his reminiscences of New York City in the 1890s, "thus providing an example to his mates of the importance of keeping his silver buttons polished and his hair brushed."

Clubs were a natural concomitant of a brownstone neighborhood. On the northeast corner of Fifth Avenue and Thirty-ninth Street was the Union League Club, founded in 1863 mainly by members of the United States Sanitary Commission, which was supported by prominent New Yorkers and soon the largest club in New York, with seventeen hundred members. The internal decoration of the very large clubhouse, built in 1888, was by the painter John La Farge and by the Tiffany firm. The entrance fee in 1893 was three hundred dollars and the annual dues seventy-five dollars.

On the southwest corner of Thirty-fifth Street was the New-York Club, and the St. Nicholas Club was at 386 Fifth Avenue (West Thirty-sixth Street). Not all the clubs were social in purpose: the Republican Club was at 450 Fifth Avenue (West Forty-fourth Street); the Democratic Club was much farther up the avenue at number 617 (East Fiftieth Street).

By the late 1880s the reservoir at West Forty-second Street, once the pride of New Yorkers, was as decayed as some of its Egyptian inspirations; furthermore, it was no longer needed as a source for clean water. The plot, measuring 455 by 420 feet, was coveted by the Metropolitan Museum of Art, the New-York Historical Society, and other institutions looking for a

Although Ulysses S. Grant
lived in New York for only a
year before his death on 23
July 1885, a splendidly solemn
funeral procession six miles
long was held on the 8th of
August after tremendous
preparation. This photograph
was taken on Fifth Avenue
below Forty-second Street.
The procession ended on the
West Side at Riverside Park,
where in 1897 the permanent
tomb was dedicated.

The New York Public Library,
designed by Carrère and
Hastings and dedicated
in 1911, dominates the important junction of Fifth Avenue
and Forty-second Street and
has long been a favorite
vantage point for New York's
major celebrations. This
photograph shows the library
decorated for the parade of
the 26th of March, 1919,
celebrating the U.S. victory
in World War I.

prime site, and by a small band of citizens who wanted it for another institution that New York City needed badly, a public library.

Readers in the city had to find books in a weird patchwork of private research libraries like the Astor on Lafayette Place and the Lenox on Fifth Avenue at Seventieth Street, private subscription libraries, "free circulating libraries" endowed by private citizens, and the libraries of various clubs and religious groups. In all, there were about three hundred libraries in the city, totally unallied and mostly open for short hours. The idea of amalgamating most of these institutions into one great free public library for both the circulation of books and research was forwarded when Samuel J. Tilden, former governor of New York and presidential candidate (he was the loser in the disputed election of 1876), and corporation lawyer, left nearly his entire estate, over five million dollars, to a trust for building a public library. His nieces and nephews did not subscribe to this noble purpose and instantly brought suit against the estate. They were successful in getting half the Tilden Trust, reducing the building fund to a little over two million dollars.

Long negotiations between the Tilden Trust, the trustees of the Astor and Lenox libraries, and representatives of free circulating libraries finally resulted in a merger in 1895. Private enterprise triumphed; city government was stingy and actively hostile to the library, which promised few patronage jobs for the incumbent Tammany Hall politicians. The congratulations exchanged among leading New Yorkers closely resembled those heard when the reservoir was opened: *Harper's Weekly* wrote, "New York is to have a public library commensurate with its population, its wealth, and its intellectual standing...."

The reservoir site was secured from the municipality, which gave with bad grace and only because of public clamor, and a design competition for the building was held: eighty-eight architectural firms submitted plans. The Beaux-Arts plan based on French Renaissance originals submitted by John M. Carrère and Thomas Hastings was selected. The cornerstone was laid in 1900. For those days construction was slow, partly because of the architects' extreme conscientiousness and attention to details; they designed not only the exterior but the interiors and fittings. The dedication of the New York Public Library was held on 23 May 1911.

The pair of life-size lions carved from pink Tennessee marble by Edward Clark Potter were placed on the Fifth Avenue side of the building at the same time. They were immediately nicknamed Patience and Fortitude. The names were not intended to be complimentary; quite a few New Yorkers thought the lions much too tame; they were unkindly described as "mealy-mouthed" and "squash-faced," neither majestic enough for the great building nor fierce enough for New York taste. In a few years, however, the amiable beasts became great favorites of New Yorkers and, next to the Statue of Liberty, the best-known sculpture in the city.

Although for most of the nineteenth century brownstones were complacently thought by New Yorkers to be perfection in domestic architecture, by the end of the century there was a reaction against them. The architectural critic Montgomery Schuyler denounced brownstones in 1899 when he wrote, "untold architectural harm was done by the malefactor who discovered that a house of brick and brownstone could be constructed, by using the stone not legitimately to bind the brickwork and span its openings but to conceal the brickwork altogether by plastering a veneer of brownstone four inches deep upon a brick wall, leaving the actual material to expose itself at the rear." Working himself into a rage, he asserted of brownstones that "to live in and among them, to become inured to them, was to suffer a depravation of taste and the more pitiable for being unconscious."

Brownstone living faded away at the end of the nineteenth century on Fifth Avenue below Fifty-ninth Street, killed not by the opinions of highbrow critics like Schuyler but by the steady advance of business. By the turn of this century the section of Fifth Avenue between Thirty-fourth and Forty-second streets, like the blocks downtown, had largely succumbed to trade. The address was the lure: if a Fifth Avenue address was a distinguished one for residences, why not for shops? B. Altman's, although the most discreet of retail establishments, led the way. The change, when it came, was astonishingly rapid, tantamount to an upheaval. Brownstones were torn down by the score and replaced with commercial establishments. The pattern was one of relatively low-rise buildings with stores and showrooms on the street level, offices and workrooms above.

In 1906 the already esteemed jewelry and decorations shop Tiffany & Co. moved from Union Square to new quarters on the southeast corner of Fifth Avenue and Thirty-seventh Street. The handsome seven-story building designed for them by McKim, Mead & White was modeled after a Venetian palace. The famous clock supported on the shoulders of a sculpted Atlas from the building at Union Square was fixed to the front of the new building, which in elegant understatement, did not carry the Tiffany name on the outside. The Fifth Avenue side of the first floor displayed jewelry and silver, while the second floor was devoted to bronze sculpture (including for years the work of Frederic Remington) and marble statuary. On the third floor were pottery and glassware; on the fourth, photography and engraving services; on the fifth, goldsmiths; on the sixth, clocks; the seventh floor was reserved for exhibitions. Tiffany's stayed at the location until 1940, when the store moved up Fifth Avenue to the southeast corner of Fifty-seventh Street, where the Atlas clock again surmounts the front door. The Thirty-seventh Street building, much neglected, to the indignation of preservationists, is still standing.

I. J. Fox, a furrier, whose store was just below Tiffany's on Fifth Avenue, became famous for his window dressing, which displayed ladies in rare furs walking through winter landscapes rather than the customary stiff display of items for sale. Later, Fox was one of the first merchants to use skywriting as an advertising device.

Best & Co., "children's outfitters," located on Fifth Avenue at West Thirty-fifth Street in 1910 and remained there until 1947, when it also moved up Fifth Avenue to Fifty-first Street. It remained there until it and fourteen branch stores closed permanently in 1970.

Next door was the Gorham Manufacturing Company, silversmiths, which opened their doors in 1906 at number 390, on the southwest corner of Thirty-sixth Street, in a Florentine building of great richness designed by McKim, Mead & White that is still standing. Lord and Taylor's department store was on the avenue between Thirty-eighth and Thirty-ninth streets from 1914 on; their building, still in operation, was designed by

Moving up from Union Square in 1906, Tiffany & Co. arrived on Fifth Avenue and the southeast corner of Thirty-seventh Street. The new building's architects, McKim, Mead & White, created a Venetian Renaissance facade in contrast to the Florentine Renaissance–style building they had built across the avenue for the rival Gorham Company. Tiffany & Co. left this building, which is still standing, moving in 1940 to the southeast corner of Fifth Avenue and Fifty-seventh Street.

the firm of Starrett and Van Vleck. Franklin Simon, opening in 1902 at number 414 between Thirty-seventh and Thirty-eighth streets, offered many services, such as made-to-order children's clothes, made-to-order underwear and hats, and a strong line in riding habits. The store also had a special department for outfitting "big women."

The Gorham Company building, on the southwest corner of Fifth Avenue and Thirty-sixth Street, was designed by Stanford White and completed in 1906. At the time, there were still a few residences in the neighborhood, but the building was surrounded primarily by such businesses as furriers, corsetieres, milliners, jewelers, and the famous "children's outfitters," Best & Co. The building survives with its street floor much renovated, but with its extraordinary cornice intact.

The Maillard Store and Restaurant opened on the southwest corner of Fifth Avenue and Thirty-fifth Street in 1908, moving uptown from the Fifth Avenue Hotel, where it had occupied a store on the street floor. Maillard confectionary had been sold in New York since 1848, when Henry Maillard arrived from France. His factory on Mercer Street was delightfully known as the Bon-Bon Building. Mabel Osgood Wright remembered from her years as a young lady that "a beau who gave Maillard's bonbons was a beau indeed, for the stamp of this shop was a guarantee that those who bought its wares were paying the greatest compliment in sweets that could be had outside of Paris." The sweetshop was so well known by the time of the Civil War that a verse published at the time read as follows:

> One night, at Maillard's cream saloon,
> As I was eating jelly
> I caught a glimpse across my spoon
> Of that gay witch, Miss Nelly.

At the Thirty-fifth Street shop, candies were displayed in what *Town & Country* magazine called "dainty French settings." There was a restaurant furnished in the Louis XVI style that had the new luxury of a refrigerating plant that promised an even temperature of seventy degrees during New York's hot summers. Although upper-class ladies did not dine out in public restaurants, they did lunch with other ladies.

In 1890 another confectioner, Louis Sherry, a Vermonter of French descent, opened his own restaurant on Fifth Avenue and Thirty-seventh Street. Its success was immediate, and it became the site of many of the famous parties of the late Gilded Age. Many were more socially awesome, but none was so deliciously salacious as "the awful Seeley party," which pleasantly diverted the public for days. On 19 December 1896, Herbert Barnum Seeley, nephew of P. T. Barnum, hired a room at Sherry's for the bachelor party of his bridegroom brother, Clinton Seeley. A report got around that the entertainment was to consist of a girl emerging from a cake "with nothing between her feet and the ceiling," as it was tastefully reported. The dancer, who called herself Little Egypt, was reputed to perform a lascivious Near Eastern dance for a fee of one thousand dollars. Captain Chapman of the police station on West Thirtieth Street decided to make his reputation as an enforcer of public morals by stopping this outrage. His reputation needed a little refurbishing since he represented the law in the "Tenderloin" district (the area between Twenty-fourth and Forty-second streets west of Fifth Avenue, thick with saloons, brothels, and gambling houses), which had a reputation for police graft without equal in New York. Chapman invaded the Seeley party with a force of his men; no Little Egypt was writhing, and the debauchery was limited to toasting the bridegroom. The police withdrew in some confusion.

All this business activity alarmed residents of the stylish neighborhood and quickly drove them out. The house of Mrs. George Ogilvie Hay, daughter of *the* Mrs. Astor, on Fifth Avenue above Thirty-fifth Street, built by Stanford White and the last of the family's houses in this part of New York, first became the Engineers' Club, then was demolished about 1908 for an office building. The Kip family house at 448 Fifth Avenue between Thirty-ninth and Fortieth streets was sold in 1911 for an astonishing seven hundred thousand dollars to make way for an office building. When Frederick W. Vanderbilt put his property on the southeast corner of Fifth Avenue and Fortieth Street up for sale in 1912, the only private houses remaining between Thirty-ninth and Forty-second streets were those of Mrs. Louis T. Hoyt, John Aspinwall Hadden, Jr., Gordon Norrie, and the Wendels. By that time the Haddens and the Norries, both well-known families in society, lived between a ladies' wear shop and an Armenian rug dealer, and the reclusive Wendels shared their block between Thirty-ninth and Fortieth with a candy store and Knox, the hatter. They were the "sole remaining residences in what a decade ago was New York's fashionable residence district, the famous Murray Hill," said *Town & Country*. Vanderbilt soon sold his house, and the Arnold Constable department store (founded in 1825) opened on its spot, where it remained until 1975. Arnold Constable was already a well-established firm. As *Town & Country* remarked, "As early as the Civil War years Aaron Arnold, a merchant from the Isle of Wight, had been selling real lace at $1,000 a yard and camel hair shawls, the mink of that day, for $1,500." The store, like others in the district, offered services that seem almost fabulous today: at Arnold Constable, there was a message book where notes and even letters could be left for friends.

Just at the time of World War I, Fifth Avenue became the country's leading fashion center. The phrase *Fifth Avenue label* became a main talking point in retailing all over the world. This success was related to the increasing mass production of clothes, "ready to wear" instead of home sewing or clothes made by a professional tailor or "the little dressmaker I know," so dear to the heart of upper-class ladies.

Two stenographers in Dorothy Parker's short story "The Standard of Living" always window-shopped on Fifth Avenue, "the ideal ground for their favorite game," which went like this: "You must suppose that somebody dies and leaves you a million dollars, cool. But there is a condition to the bequest. It is stated in the will that you must spend every nickel of the money on yourself." So the stenographers carefully study Fifth Avenue windows to calculate how far their million will stretch and are bewildered to find one necklace they admired in a window priced at two hundred fifty thousand dollars.

The opening of the enormous and majestic Grand Central Terminal on East Forty-second Street in 1913 made the neighborhood even more attractive to merchants and shoppers. The foresighted had realized when construction began in 1903 that major improvement in the station's vicinity would result, and soon. Although a railroad station for the New York Central Railroad had existed on East Forty-second Street since 1871, the new station, handling five hundred or more trains a day, both long-distance and suburban, gave a quick stimulus to business in the area. Its dignity and efficiency were inviting, as were its swift connections with the subway lines. Effects were quick and dramatic: numerous new hotels, office buildings, and stores, mostly of the best quality, were constructed in the neighborhood straightaway. Fifth Avenue between Thirty-fourth and Forty-second streets, an easy walk from Grand Central, attracted new waves of shoppers from the suburbs and out of town.

In the 1930s lower-priced stores began to invade the neighborhood, more a sign of the Great Depression than of any real change in Fifth Avenue. Even Kress and Woolworth wanted a share in the prestige of Fifth Avenue. The S. H. Kress and Company store, carrying goods priced at "5-, 10-, and 25-cents," was built in 1935 on the site of the Wendel house. There was some dismay that a five-and-ten would pollute this expensive section of Fifth Avenue, but the store prospered, so four years later across the street the firm's great rival, Woolworth's, built a handsome store where the Union League Club had stood. Kress was the first store to put show windows on the second floor so that passengers on the top of double-decker buses would have something to see. The southwest corner of Thirty-seventh Street was owned by the Goelet family, next to the Astors the leading real-estate dynasty in New York City. In 1914, Stewart & Company, a major new department store, had Warren & Wetmore design a new building on the site, which was 402 Fifth Avenue. The brick facade was decorated with an unusual terra-cotta design in blue and white. Stewart remained there until 1928, when it moved to Fifty-sixth Street. While shopping in the neighborhood you could lunch at one of the two restaurants run by Park & Tilford, the fancy grocers, which during the 1930s served ladies' lunches for a dollar and twenty-five cents.

In 1929 the city declared this midtown district a special retail zoning district, recognizing its importance. The ordinance connected with this declaration was that any new building put up on Fifth Avenue must devote at least the two lowest floors to stores. For reasons that are now obscure, the east side of Fifth Avenue was more fashionable for strolling than the west side: the east was known as the fifty-cent side, the west as the twenty-five-cent side. Dorothy Parker's girls, for example, would have concentrated their window-shopping on the east side of the avenue.

In the 1930s there was a rage for tearooms, a heritage of the Prohibition years. In 1934, Dawn Powell, whose New York novels are among the twentieth century's most carefully observed, dropped in at the Gypsy Tea Room on Fifth Avenue and Thirty-eighth Street. The waitresses, although not gypsies, answered to "gypsy" names like Ramona or Juanita. After lunch (and included in the price), she had a palm reading by a fortune-teller inexplicably called Ralph the White Hunter. Lunch and a reading cost seventy-five cents.

5

The Moral Landscape

Forty-second Street to Fifty-ninth Street

•

Isolated hospitals and orphanages loomed in the bleak landscape above Forty-second Street even before the Civil War. They were built there, well out of sight of most New Yorkers, largely because the municipal authorities granted land to charitable institutions for the construction of new buildings. The city could afford to be generous since the land was essentially worthless; no one seriously believed the inhabited city would ever extend so far. The charity institutions were freestanding buildings mainly located between Forty-eighth and Fifty-fifth streets both east and west of Fifth Avenue. The New York Institute for the Instruction of the Deaf and Dumb, built in 1852 and the first such institution in the United States, was on the southeast corner of Fiftieth Street and Fifth Avenue; a block north was the Catholic Orphan Asylum; the Episcopal St. Luke's Hospital was on the west side of Fifth Avenue between Fifty-fourth and Fifty-fifth streets; and the Colored Orphan Asylum was on the west side of the avenue between Forty-third and Forty-fourth streets—it was burned during the Civil War draft riots on 13 July 1863. In 1858 the construction of St. Patrick's Cathedral between Fiftieth and Fifty-first streets was begun on land sold by the city to the Roman Catholic archdiocese for one dollar.

The recipients of municipal charity occupied an unattractive and even melancholy area. Before Central Park was built, the streets above Fifty-ninth were mere tracks. Upper Fifth Avenue was described by one commentator as "a muddy dirt road which ran alongside a bog."

Episcopalians built St. Luke's Hospital on the west side of Fifth Avenue between Fifty-fourth and Fifty-fifth streets on land donated by the city when the area was largely unsettled. The hospital, completed in 1858 after four years of construction, gradually found itself hemmed in by houses as the area became fashionable: houses owned by the Vanderbilt family lay to the north and south of the hospital by 1890. In 1896, St Luke's moved to Amsterdam Avenue and West 113th Street, and the University Club and Gotham Hotel were later built on its Fifth Avenue site.

Construction on St. Patrick's Cathedral, on the east side of Fifth Avenue between Fiftieth and Fifty-first streets, began in 1858. The building was dedicated, after some delay during the Civil War, in 1879, and there were many later additions, including the spires in 1888. The architect, *James Renwick, who earlier designed Grace Church at Broadway and Twelfth Street, was inspired by the Cologne Cathedral, and St. Patrick's was an immediately impressive landmark in the low-rise neighborhood.*

Very modest refreshment and amusement were offered on the southeast corner of Forty-fourth Street at the Willow Tree Inn, owned by Tom Hyer, a noted pugilist and brawler more violent out of the ring than in and famous for wrecking the brothels where he relaxed. The Willow Tree was remarkably resistant to change, lasting until 1905, when it was demolished, unlamented by its neighbors although presumably regretted by its habitués. Newspapers called it "the last bar on Fifth Avenue" and "an eye-sore." *Town & Country* magazine remarked haughtily that there were "no associations connected with the Willow Tree."

The only exception in the generally depressing landscape was the Elgin Botanic Garden established in 1801 by Dr. David Hosack on twenty acres where Rockefeller Center now stands. Hosack was a professor of botany at Columbia College, very active in the city's cultural affairs and notable in his time as the physician who attended the duelists Alexander Hamilton and Aaron Burr at their celebrated encounter in 1804. The purpose of the garden was not decorative; it was to provide medicinal plants for study and use by medical students and was the first public botanical garden in the United States. Its botanists helped to identify the numerous unfamiliar plants collected by Meriwether Lewis and William Clark during their western explorations.

Hosack was popular with the medical students: every year he gave a strawberry festival for them in his garden. Securing rare plants and maintaining them was expensive; by 1810 Hosack was unable to bear the cost any longer. He sold his twenty acres to the state of New York, which four years later granted them to Columbia College. Until 1985, the college profitably leased the land to various other parties, including tenement houses and theaters and, from 1929 to 1985, to John D. Rockefeller, Jr., for Rockefeller Center. The college itself never occupied the space; in 1857 it moved from downtown to Madison Avenue between Forty-ninth and Fiftieth streets, where it stayed until 1897, when it moved to Morningside Heights.

In addition to charitable institutions, unattractive industries found homes above Forty-second Street: slaughterhouses, for example, between Fourth and Fifth avenues from Forty-fourth to Forty-sixth streets. A herd of cattle being driven to their fate across Fifth Avenue was not an unusual sight. The smell of the slaughterhouses and stockyards was detectable for many blocks. Before the Civil War the public pound for stray animals was at East Fifty-fifth Street. As Fifth Avenue developed these industries were pushed toward the two rivers—slaughterhouses, for example, were located where the United Nations now stands—joining other unattractive industries, such as the tanning of hides and the rendering of fat into tallow. For obvious reasons, this led New Yorkers to avoid their riverfronts.

New York City's prosperity was built on waterborne traffic. In colonial times, well-to-do New Yorkers had built fine houses along the rivers, especially country houses that caught the breezes and were regarded as healthier than the downtown city. From the mid-nineteenth century on, however, the riverbanks became increasingly polluted, crowded, and unappealing, and New Yorkers who had the choice avoided them altogether. It was not until the building of Riverside Drive, East End Avenue, the Franklin D. Roosevelt Drive along the East River, and the housing and institutional developments of the mid-twentieth century that the riverfronts were sufficiently attractive for New Yorkers to build along them once more.

The Episcopal St. Thomas Church on the northwest corner of Fifty-third Street was one of the major projects of the post–Civil War era in the neighborhood. Designed by Richard Upjohn, the church stood from 1870 to 1905, when it burned. It was rebuilt in much the same style by the architectural firm of Cram, Goodhue, and Ferguson and consecrated in 1916. The then-minister, Rev. E. M. Stires, took an obsessive interest in the design and made frequent changes; some of the plans were redrawn four or five times. He was determined to build as medievally as was possible in early twentieth-century New York: even the elevator was Gothic, and there were many statues. Most architectural critics have thought the yellow sandstone interior more successful than the exterior and have praised the wood carvings by Lee Lawrie on the church furniture.

The Fifth Avenue Presbyterian Church, formerly at Nineteenth Street, moved to the northwest corner of Fifth Avenue and Fifty-fifth Street in 1875, where it remains. At 551 Fifth Avenue, near Forty-fifth Street, was the Church of the Heavenly Rest, built in 1868 by the architect Edward Tuckerman Potter; the parish originated in services held in the hall of Rutgers Female College in 1865. At Forty-fifth Street it had only a narrow entrance between two small office buildings. The Collegiate Reformed Church, also known as the Church of St. Nicholas, was an ancient congregation descended from the Dutch church within the fort

The first St. Thomas's Episcopal Church, on the northwest corner of Fifth Avenue and Fifty-third Street, was dedicated in 1870. Designed by Richard Upjohn, the architect of Trinity Church, at Broadway and Wall Street, and the Church of the Ascension, at Fifth Avenue and Tenth Street, the church attracted an increasingly wealthy congregation as more town houses were built in the neighborhood. The original structure burned in 1905 and was replaced by the present church, designed by Ralph Adams Cram in 1906.

in Peter Stuyvesant's New York. From 1859 it stood on the northwest corner of Fifth Avenue and Forty-eighth Street.

Not all the ecclesiastical structures were Christian. Temple Emanu-El, a Reform Jewish congregation, stood on the northeast corner of Fifth Avenue and Forty-third Street from 1867. It was built by Leopold Eidlitz in the Moorish style. It was the first Reform congregation in New York City. Eidlitz was born in Prague and came to this country in 1843. He had previously designed St. George's Episcopal Church in Stuyvesant Square and had a hand in designing the New York County ("Tweed") Courthouse. Temple Emanu-El merged with Temple Beth-El in 1928.

By far the largest ecclesiastical structure was St. Patrick's, the cathedral church of the archdiocese of New York. James Renwick, the architect of Grace Church and, incidentally, a Protestant and senior warden of Grace Church, designed it in the Gothic Revival style, basing his designs on the German Cathedral of Cologne. Construction was much more rapid than that of medieval cathedrals and even of the Episcopal Cathedral of St. John the Divine in New York: St. Patrick's was begun in 1858 and dedicated in 1879; St. John the Divine was begun in 1892 and is today far from finished. St. Patrick's cost 1.9 million dollars to build; spires added in 1888 cost an additional two hundred thousand dollars. The isolation of its site when it was built and the lack of nearby tall buildings added to the impressiveness of St. Patrick's, which could be seen for miles at the time. Its presence was the physical assertion of a major change in the city's population. The largest and handsomest churches in New York had always been Protestant; the size and splendor of St. Patrick's, and especially its location on Fifth Avenue, marked the enormous increase and growing political importance of the city's immigrant and Catholic population.

Excluding shanties and workmen's huts, there were hardly any residences on Fifth Avenue in the section while St. Patrick's was being built. The striking exception was on the northeast corner of Fifth Avenue and Fifty-seventh Street, where the houses known as Marble Row were built for Mrs. Isaac Jones (Mary Mason) by the architect Robert Mook between 1867 and 1869. Mary Mason Jones was an heiress married to a rich man; the family owned the important Chemical Bank.

Marble Row consisted of five houses between Fifty-seventh and Fifty-eighth streets, each with its own entrance. Mary Mason Jones was obviously a woman of spirit; when she built her marble houses just after the Civil War, they went up in an area where the streets had only just been laid out and very few buildings were to be seen. She evidently felt from the

beginning that the city would catch up with her, and of course it did, although there must have been some discouraging years of isolation when friends and relatives were unwilling to go so far uptown. Mrs. Paran Stevens rented the house on the northeast corner of Fifty-seventh Street, always known as 1 East Fifty-seventh; Vanderbilts, Whitneys, and Huntingtons soon clustered around Fifth Avenue and Fifty-seventh Street; and Mary Mason Jones's sister-in-law, Mrs. Colford Jones, built two marble houses between Fifty-fifth and Fifty-sixth streets in 1869.

The houses of Marble Row fascinated contemporaries, and even though they were torn down by 1930, they have continued to fascinate

"Marble Row" consisted of five French chateau–style houses along the east side of Fifth Avenue between Fifty-seventh and Fifty-eighth Streets. Designed by Robert Mook, and built between 1867 and 1869 for Mrs. Isaac Jones (who defiantly referred to herself as Mrs. Mary Mason Jones), the wife of the president of the Chemical Bank, the houses were regarded as among the finest residences in New York. Mrs. Jones occupied the house on the corner of Fifth Avenue and Fifty-seventh Street and leased the others. The Warner Brothers store is now in a 1930 building on the corner.

history-minded New Yorkers. They have particular interest for readers of Edith Wharton: Mary Mason Jones was Wharton's aunt by marriage, and she makes an unforgettable appearance as Mrs. Mingott in *The Age of Innocence*. Marble Row was replaced by 745 Fifth Avenue, longtime home of the beloved toy store F. A. O. Schwarz.

Above Forty-second Street, new residences tended to be larger than those from Thirty-fourth to Forty-second streets but usually were brownstone, too. On the southeast corner of Fifth Avenue and Forty-third Street the brownstone at number 511 was the residence of William M. "Boss" Tweed, who bought it with the adjacent vacant lot, a total sixty-two-foot frontage on Fifth Avenue, for $275,000. Tweed's daughter was married from this house during his reign in city government, or *mis*government. The wedding gifts, which included diamond necklaces and other jewels, were stupendous, and the newspapers took great pleasure in enumerating them, along with their probable cost. Most came from politicians and from cronies for whom he had done favors. Tweed did not enjoy his prosperity for long. In 1876 he was arrested for stealing millions from the city's treasury. He was jailed but requested permission to return to 511 Fifth Avenue to pick up some clothes. There, he eluded his guards, reached his yacht anchored in the East River, and sailed off to Florida, Cuba, and then Spain. The flight was obviously carefully planned and, equally obvious, was assisted by powerful people in the city anxious to ward off any public confessions he might make. The plan worked only temporarily. Spain extradited Tweed back to New York, where he was tried and convicted. He died in prison in 1878.

Tweed's valuable Fifth Avenue property was sold four years later to Richard T. Wilson, a Tennessee Confederate who had made a fortune selling Southern cotton abroad during the Civil War and had developed social ambitions for his children. He and his clever wife moved to New York to forward them. The Wilson house was far from being a mansion; it was rather poky and was already being surrounded by businesses, but the parents were amiable hosts and the children of the household immediately became popular. They were unusually attractive, and the results of the Wilsons' social campaign were spectacular, one of the great triumphs in the history of nineteenth-century American society: a son

The Fifth Avenue Bank opened in a former town house on the northwest corner of Fifth Avenue and Forty-fourth Street in 1890, which was then a fashionable location: Delmonico's was across Fifth Avenue and Sherry's was across Forty-fourth Street. The bank service was legendary, especially for its solicitude toward the rich ladies in the neighborhood, who included Mrs. Robert Goelet, the real estate heiress; Mrs. Russell Sage, widow of the financier; and the Duchess of Talleyrand, daughter of Jay Gould.

married an Astor; a daughter married a Vanderbilt; another, a Goelet; and the last, the son of the Earl of Pembroke. The Wilson house was demolished in 1915.

Nearby, Jay Gould, the railroad manipulator and accumulator of companies, lived at a large house at 578 Fifth Avenue, on the northwest corner of Forty-seventh Street, from 1870 to 1882, when he moved across the street to number 579. At the time he first moved to Fifth Avenue, Gould was already considered the "most hated man in America"; his speculations in the Erie and other railroads and his attempt to corner the gold market had ruined hundreds of people. Few of the victims could be described as widows and orphans, being for the most part equally greedy but not so skillful speculators, but Gould was held responsible for pauperizing families. He suffered from stomach troubles—small wonder—and chronic insomnia. He could be seen pacing the sidewalk on Fifth Avenue in front of number 579, flanked by two bodyguards, night after night, trying to get tired enough to sleep.

Jay Gould's eldest son, George Jay Gould, favored child and principal manager of the vast Gould properties after his father died, married in 1884. His bride was an actress, Edith Kingdon, more renowned for her looks than her theatrical talent. George's conservative mother took to her bed at the thought of an actress daughter-in-law, but Jay took the marriage calmly and gave the couple a house next door at 1 East Forty-seventh Street and built a passage connecting it with his own house.

Jay Gould's daughter Helen Miller Gould Shepard inherited her father's house. She preserved it exactly the way it was when her father lived there, as she also preserved Lyndhurst, his country home at Tarrytown. The furnishings of the Fifth Avenue house remained Victorian until the middle of the twentieth century: the windows on Fifth Avenue hung with multiple layers of curtains, the walls covered with tapestries, and every flat surface teeming with family photographs.

Helen Miller Gould Shepard, who did not marry until she was middle-aged, was a busybody, constantly giving instructions to the exasperated management of the numerous railroads she and her siblings had inherited. She was philanthropic but naive and conventional to the point of simplemindedness. She was a generous patron of charities and institutions, some of them legitimate (New York University) and some tenuous (a society for the "alleviation" of polygamous Mormon wives), and was surrounded at all times by missionaries. Family and guests were expected to have apt biblical quotations ready at all times. No liquor was ever served in her homes. She adopted four children, two of whom had been left as foundlings on the steps of nearby St. Patrick's Cathedral. They were schooled and sent to church and became quick with Bible verses. Although self-centered and remote and by no means an attentive mother,

Helen Miller Gould Shepard insisted that each child kiss her on entering and leaving any room where she was sitting; one weary child estimated that she was kissed between thirty and forty times every day. In 1942, when it was virtually the only brownstone left on Fifth Avenue below Fifty-ninth Street, the Gould house was leased to Gimbel Brothers, whose Kende Galleries branch held auctions of art and jewelry there until 1952, when it was finally demolished.

Of prurient interest to passersby in this generally ultrarespectable neighborhood was the stately house at 657 Fifth Avenue, home of "Madame Restell." Madame Restell, whose name was really Caroline Ann (Trow) Somers Lohman, was an English-born immigrant who was New York City's busiest and best-known abortionist from the 1840s on. She lacked even rudimentary medical training and was greedy and irresponsible. Her career, though profitable, was marked by horrifying scandals, including accusations of murder, procuring, and blackmail. She spent occasional short terms in the "Tombs," New York's municipal jail, but a combination of bribery and skillful lawyers kept her free most of the time. She and her second husband, Charles Lohman, a successful real-estate speculator, bought ten lots on the east side of Fifth Avenue between Fifty-second and Fifty-third streets for $36,500 in 1864 and built a large house on the northeast corner of Fifty-second Street, supposed to have cost, with furnishings, $200,000. "The whole house is filled with statuettes, paintings, rare bronzes, ornamental and valuable clocks, candelabras, silver globes and articles of virtu," wrote a reporter lucky enough to penetrate the pretentious establishment, which also served as Madame Restell's "office." The window shades were especially admired, as well they might be, as each was painted by a leading artist at a fee said to be $1,000 per shade.

The Lohmans had some difficulty in selling the other lots they owned; as Madame's appearances wearing loads of jewelry and riding in a superb carriage became ever more flamboyant and shameless, people did not want to live next door to her. Finally, an apartment building called the Osborne (the first of several of that name) was built on the lots north of her house. Madame Restell's downfall came in 1878, when she encountered the tireless Anthony Comstock of the New York Society for the Suppression of Vice, who arrested her for selling abortifacients. While

In 1879, William H. Vanderbilt II, having inherited the better part of $100 million from his father, Cornelius Vanderbilt, purchased the blockfront on the west side of Fifth Avenue between Fifty-first and Fifty-second streets for an unprecedented $700,000. The double house he built, one wing for himself and his wife, the other for their daughters, was not admired for its exterior (compared to packing boxes), but the interiors, by the great decorating firm of the Herter Brothers, were splendid.

Suppression of Vice, who arrested her for selling abortifacients. While the case was pending she committed suicide.

No family ever built more grandly on Fifth Avenue than the Vanderbilts. When Commodore Vanderbilt, who lived modestly near Washington Square while making himself the richest man in America with steamships and railroads, died in 1877, leaving an estate of about one hundred million dollars, his descendants, hitherto equally modest in their living arrangements, almost immediately began planning new townhouses, most of them on Fifth Avenue; no other address seems to have been considered.

The first was the double house built by William Henry Vanderbilt, the Commodore's eldest son, for himself and his daughters on a plot on the west side of Fifth Avenue between Fifty-first and Fifty-third streets. The

location had humble beginnings in a truck farm owned by Frederick Beinhauer, a German immigrant who bought this plot, then rural, in 1800. He died in 1823, and his land passed through other hands before Vanderbilt bought it. William Henry's house was number 640; at number 642 he built a house for his daughter Emily and her husband, William Douglas Sloane, and adjoining at 2 West Fifty-second Street, another for daughter Margaret and her husband, Elliott F. Shepard. In a few years daughter Florence Adele and her husband, Hamilton McKown Twombly, built at 684 Fifth Avenue, and Lila Vanderbilt, still another daughter, and her husband, William Seward Webb, moved into 680 Fifth Avenue, next door to St. Thomas's Church.

William Henry's house was a brownstone with family quarters (there was only William Henry, his wife, Maria Louisa Kissam, and their youngest

No more imposing site for a town house in New York existed in the 1880s than the intersection of Fifth Avenue and Fifty-seventh Street. On the northwest corner, across from Marble Row and a block from Grand Army Plaza, Cornelius Vanderbilt II and his wife, Alice Gwynne Vanderbilt, built the most splendid of all the Vanderbilt town houses. The Bergdorf-Goodman store is there now.

child, George) on the first two floors, the servants' rooms on the third, and storerooms on the fourth. The central hall, three stories in height, was skylighted and led into a picture gallery where the Vanderbilts' collection of contemporary French paintings was hung (and open to the public on certain days). The unforgettable feature of the central hall was a malachite vase nine feet tall, originally a gift from the tsar of Russia to Prince Demidoff (and now in the Metropolitan Museum of Art). The entire house was furnished with purchases made by the Vanderbilts on their frequent trips to Europe, not only paintings, but furniture, ceramics, and glass. The arrangement of these objects was entrusted to the firm of Herter Brothers, furniture makers and interior decorators.

The houses of William Henry Vanderbilt and his daughters were not nearly the end of Vanderbilt ambitions in the neighborhood, only the first in a series of Vanderbilt mansions that extended six blocks up Fifth Avenue. William K. Vanderbilt, William Henry's son, had Richard Morris Hunt design the most striking of the Vanderbilt houses at 660 Fifth Avenue, the northwest corner of Fifty-second Street. In the richest François I style, the house was the setting for the Vanderbilt ball of 26 March 1883, a costume party attended by most of the major figures in New York society, including the Astors, who had long resisted the blandishments of the Vanderbilts but finally succumbed to the temptation of attending the housewarming ball at number 660.

Next door, at 666 Fifth Avenue, the southwest corner of Fifty-third Street, William K. Vanderbilt's son, William K., Jr., and his wife, Virginia Graham Fair, had McKim, Mead & White design for them another François I house, notable for its historicity and dignity. While up on the northwest corner of Fifth Avenue and Fifty-seventh Street his uncle Cornelius Vanderbilt II and his wife, Alice Gwynne, occupied the largest of the Vanderbilt New York houses, designed by the architect George B. Post in what was called, rather loosely, "a seventeenth century French style." With "Vanderbilt Row" from Fifty-first to Fifty-seventh streets and the houses of their kin scattered along the avenue and nearby side streets, the Vanderbilts made an impact on Fifth Avenue unequaled even by the "cave-dwelling" Knickerbocker families around Washington Square.

At 719 Fifth Avenue, between East Fifty-fifth and Fifty-sixth streets, lived George Gustav Heye, son of a prosperous German-American immigrant who had founded an oil refining company and a lady who was descended from Colonel Richard E. Lawrence, one of the founders of King's College (later Columbia). The carriage house for this residence still exists on East Sixty-ninth Street between Lexington and Third avenues. Heye was six feet four inches tall and weighed three hundred pounds. He graduated from the Columbia School of Mines but was always more interested in collecting and research into ancient cultures than in his profession. He and his mother sponsored a series of archaeological expeditions to Mexico and South America beginning in 1904, and his wife also shared his enthusiasms. In 1915 he set up the Heye Foundation. His collections became the Museum of the American Indian on Audubon Terrace on Broadway at 155th Street, built in 1916 and opened to the public in 1922. Heye was a boxcar collector, so-called because he bought Indian artifacts by the boxcar. One bemused friend said he "would be fretful and hard to live with until he'd bought every last dirty dishcloth and discarded shoe and shipped them back to New York. He felt he couldn't conscientiously leave a reservation until its entire population was practically naked…."

Harvard was the first college to have its own quarters in New York City; the Harvard Club opened in 1865. The same year a band of men from various colleges began meeting for dinner. In 1879 the group organized as the University Club. Membership was wide: any man was eligible who had graduated from a college or university or from the military or naval academies; even holders of honorary degrees could join. Membership at the end of the nineteenth century was limited to thirty-five hundred, of which about two hundred were Army or Navy men.

In 1899 the club built new quarters on Fifth Avenue at the northwest corner of Fifty-fourth Street (the address has always been 1 West Fifty-fourth Street). The best American talents were employed in the design: the building in the grandest Italian Renaissance style was designed by Charles Follen McKim; a frieze at the top of the seven-story building was decorated with the seals of eighteen colleges designed by the sculptor

The University Club, although having one of the largest memberships of any men's club in the city, was homeless for long periods after its founding in 1865. Once they decided to build a clubhouse of their own, however, the members spared no expense, commissioning McKim, Mead & White to design their headquarters. When their new Italian Renaissance—style building on the northwest corner of Fifth Avenue and Fifty-fourth Street opened in 1899, the organization boasted that it was "the finest club-house in the world."

Daniel Chester French. A century later it remains by general acclaim one of the finest buildings on Fifth Avenue.

In 1903 the Union Club moved to the northeast corner of Fifth Avenue and Fifty-first Street, formerly the site of the Catholic Orphanage. There was good reason for moving uptown: a survey of members showed that only 17 percent lived below Twenty-third Street and only 7 percent between Twenty-third and Thirty-fourth streets.

Number 512, the southwest corner of Forty-third Street, was the Hotel Renaissance. Among its distinguished tenants were William Rutherford Mead of the great architectural firm of McKim, Mead & White; David H. King, Jr., the builder who erected the King Model Houses in 1891 in Harlem on West 138th and 139th streets, some of which were designed by McKim, Mead & White, known when Harlem's population became largely black after World War I as Strivers' Row; Carl Schurz, the German-American senator and newspaperman whose name is commemorated in the park on East Eighty-sixth Street; and Ernest Thompson Seton, the naturalist and founder of the Woodcraft League for boys, whose *Wild Animals I Have Known* was an 1898 best-seller. His Renaissance Hotel rooms were decorated with animal skins.

After John King, president of the Erie Railroad, was blackballed from membership in the Union Club for his primitive table manners, J. P. Morgan and other friends of King formed the Metropolitan Club in 1891. The clubhouse, designed by Stanford White, opened on the northeast corner of Fifth Avenue and Sixty-first Street in 1894. The tables shown here are laid for one of the club's dinners; the roses heaped in the center prevented talking across the table, which was considered rude.

At 556 Fifth Avenue, near Forty-sixth Street, M. Knoedler & Co., art dealers, put up a spacious and highly decorative art gallery designed by Carrère & Hastings in limestone with ground-floor stonework when the firm moved uptown from Fifth Avenue and Thirty-fourth Street. Knoedler's rival, René Gimpel, who dealt in single, very expensive pictures and had the advantage over Knoedler of keeping a diary for posterity, wrote disdainfully, "This place is a bazaar." A customer could spend a hundred dollars on a painting by a contemporary artist or a hundred thousand on an old master or five dollars on a print. Knoedler's also cleaned paintings and framed them. Knoedler's stayed at the address only until 1925, when it moved to East Fifty-seventh Street, which had by that time become the most popular area in New York for art dealers. Number 556 became a popular Schrafft's restaurant for the next twenty-five years.

René Gimpel himself had his office at 647 Fifth Avenue, a five-story marble-facade private mansion next door to Cartier. "Three windows facing the street," he wrote in his diary; "here that's a lot, since multimillionaires usually have only two—a tough country."

Sherry's moved just seven blocks uptown and opened on Fifth Avenue and the southwest corner of Forty-fourth Street the second week in October 1898. A few months later, in the spring of 1899, its rival, Delmonico's, opened on the northeast corner. The new Sherry's was a twelve-story restaurant and apartment hotel designed by Stanford White. The apartments were originally intended for single men, but later, a few married couples lived there. One of the longtime tenants was the bachelor publisher Frank Munsey, who came in 1898 and stayed until Sherry's closed in 1919. He was a former grocer who became one of the strangest figures in the history of American newspaper publishing: he seemed to buy newspapers for the pleasure of closing them down. In New York City alone he killed four. After he died in 1925, William Allen White wrote of his career, "Frank Munsey contributed to the journalism of his day the talent of a meat packer, the morals of a money changer, and the manners of an undertaker." Munsey's eccentricities were famous: he had an aversion to balloons and such a frantic hatred of fat men that overweight members of his staff used to hide in closets when he visited his office in the Flatiron Building. The journalist Arthur Brisbane described his rooms

The rise of Louis Sherry,
restaurateur and caterer, was
astonishing even in the
get-rich-quick New York of the
late nineteenth century.
In 1881, he opened a small
restaurant on Sixth Avenue;
in 1890, he bought a
house at Fifth Avenue and
Thirty-seventh Street owned
by the Goelet family; and in
1898, he built this twelve-story
building designed by Stanford
White on the northwest
corner of Fifth Avenue and
Forty-fourth Street.

the Flatiron Building. The journalist Arthur Brisbane described his rooms at Sherry's as "the coldest spot outside the Arctic Circle."

As for the restaurant, after Sherry's moved uptown it became palmier than ever. In his novel *Sister Carrie*, published in 1900, Theodore Dreiser portrayed the dining room as a scene of Babylonian splendor. Carrie, recently arrived in New York and poor, is taken by spendthrift new friends to Sherry's for dinner.

> Here was the place where the matter of expense limited the patrons to the moneyed or pleasure-loving class.... Incandescent lights, the reflection of their glow in polished glasses, and the shine of gilt upon the walls combined into one tone of light which it requires minutes of complacent observation to separate and take particular note of.... The floor was of reddish hue, waxed and polished, and in every direction were mirrors— tall, brilliant, bevel-edge mirrors—reflecting and re-reflecting forms, faces, and candelabra a score and a hundred times.

According to Dreiser and other observers, "The large bill of fare held an array of dishes sufficient to feed an army, sidelined with prices which made reasonable expenditure a ridiculous impossibility...." Oysters cost sixty cents a half dozen. Soup, of which a dozen kinds were offered, was fifty cents.

The Windsor Hotel, built in 1873, stood on the east side of Fifth Avenue between Forty-sixth and Forty-seventh streets. Among its longtime residents were Mr. and Mrs. Andrew Carnegie, who lived there before they built their own Fifth Avenue house. The hotel was totally destroyed by fire on 17 March 1899 while the St. Patrick's Day parade was passing in front. Twenty lives were lost. It was replaced by the Windsor Arcade, one of the grandest retail buildings in New York, containing mainly bookshops, china and glass stores, and small art galleries. Also in the arcade were Pach Brothers, the famous portrait photographers, and Steinway & Sons, pianos. Despite the elegance of the arcade and its tenants, the neighbors, who held the prevailing views about commerce on Fifth Avenue, which they correctly saw as advancing steadily onto their ground, protested loudly against its construction. No doubt to their satisfaction, the three-story arcade was never particularly successful although it lasted until 1920.

Stately residences, churches, and clubs having reached as far north as Grand Army Plaza at Fifth Avenue and Fifty-ninth Street, hotels were sure to follow. The southeast entrance to Central Park was an obviously

The Windsor Arcade was one of several attempts around 1900 to create a London-style enclosed street of shops in New York. The two-story arcade was built on the site of the Windsor Hotel, which had burned in 1899, on the east side of Fifth Avenue between Forty-sixth and Forty-seventh streets. The arcade was never very successful—perhaps an early indication of New Yorkers' general aversion to malls—and was demolished in 1920.

The second hotel named the Plaza on the superb site facing Grand Army Plaza to the east and Central Park to the north always welcomed transient guests, but, like its predecessor, was also home to permanent residents. The first guests, Mr. and Mrs. Alfred Gwynne Vanderbilt, took an apartment when they signed the register in 1907.

convenient and conspicuous location. On the west side of the plaza on a spot that once was a pond used for ice skating, the Plaza Hotel was opened in 1890. The architects were McKim, Mead & White, but the hotel was not considered one of their best efforts. By 1905 it was torn down. As one commentator said unkindly, "It was a huge barn and its disappearance was a matter of congratulation." A new Plaza Hotel with

about eight hundred rooms was designed by Henry J. Hardenbergh and opened in 1907.

Across Fifth Avenue on the southeast corner of Fifty-ninth Street was the Hotel Savoy (number 767). The history of the site was intriguing. As early as 1870, Boss Tweed had decided the site was the finest in the city for a new hotel and for the investment of the loot he had acquired during his reign as lord of the city treasury; he began excavations for a building he planned to call The Knickerbocker. Tweed's fall meant that The Knickerbocker never got built. The plot remained a vacant eyesore until the twelve-story Hotel Savoy, designed by Ralph S. Townsend, was built and opened in 1892. The public rooms were embellished with an array

In 1892, two large hotels opened at Fifty-ninth Street on the east side of Grand Army Plaza: the New Netherland (left) and the Savoy (right). Both were largely residential, reflecting a strong tradition in New York of the rich making their homes in hotels, securing deluxe service without servant problems. Transient visitors usually stayed further downtown at the Astor House or the Waldorf-Astoria. The sites are now occupied by the Sherry-Netherland hotel and the General Motors building.

of marbles that must have been absolutely dazzling. The state suite (also known as the bridal suite) on the second floor was a reproduction of the boudoir of Marie Antoinette at the Petit Trianon in Versailles. Although referred to as a hotel, the Savoy was actually a luxury apartment house with more-or-less permanent residents. They included in 1914 Charles H. Hayden; Roland F. Knoedler, the art dealer; and Mrs. Rhinelander Waldo, who had just built an extraordinary Renaissance house on the southeast corner of Madison Avenue and Seventy-second Street but did not live in it.

Developments such as these near Central Park had been foreseen, and not encouragingly, by New York's own good gray poet William Cullen Bryant. Bryant edited the *New York Evening Post* from 1829 to almost the time of his death in 1878. Distinguished as a poet (one of his best-known works is "Thanatopsis") before he became an editor, he encouraged so many good causes (Central Park, public health, the Metropolitan Museum of Art) that he became the most influential man in New York and the calm recipient of municipal adulation. As he grew older the incense rather went to his head and he became increasingly oracular in his public statements. In 1878, while he was crossing Fifth Avenue at Grand Army Plaza, he looked at the new buildings rising on Fifty-ninth Street, and remarked, or rather declared, "They have covered the earth and now they are reaching up to the clouds…this beautiful Park, this gift, blended by nature and art, to the people of New York, may be surrounded on all sides by buildings eight, nay possibly ten stories in height, until the spirit of the Park's loveliness, will go from it."

Traffic was becoming appalling, as more and more automobiles appeared on the streets. There were lots of pedestrian accidents: even Winston Churchill on a trip to New York was knocked down by an automobile while crossing Fifth Avenue. There were no traffic lights until 1919, when the first was put up at Fifth Avenue and Forty-second Street. After 1904 a series of traffic regulations came into force, and policemen were stationed at the busiest intersections to direct traffic; they were expected to help ladies and children across the streets by holding up the traffic. Around the same time, Police Commissioner William McAdoo introduced the first equestrian policemen. William P. Eno originated the one-way street, rotary traffic—first put into effect at Columbus Circle in 1905—and safety islands. In 1908, Fifth Avenue was widened, eliminating many front areas, trees, and stoops in response to the increasing traffic. The effect was to remove the last vestiges of rurality along Fifth Avenue, which had been preserved for an astonishingly long time.

After making his fortune in California railroads, Collis P. Huntington moved to New York and in 1892 commissioned George B. Post, architect of the Cornelius Vanderbilt II house diagonally across Fifth Avenue, to design his "Romanesque" mansion on the southeast corner of Fifty-seventh Street. The press, invited to tour the house upon its completion, were particularly fascinated by Mrs. Huntington's extravagant bathtub, which they called "Diana's Pool" and "the most famous bath in the world." Tiffany's is now on this corner.

In the 1920s, the last residences around Fifth Avenue and Fifty-seventh Street vanished to make room for an influx of businesses. The flamboyant full-block residence of Cornelius Vanderbilt II on the west side of Fifth Avenue between Fifty-seventh and Fifty-eighth streets was demolished in 1926 and replaced in 1928 with an extant complex of elegant shops anchored on the southwest corner of Fifty-eighth Street by the Bergdorf-Goodman store.

The first sight-seeing buses invaded Fifth Avenue in the 1890s. The sport was then known inelegantly as rubbernecking. Tourists rode in a retired Fifth Avenue stage with two horses; eventually seats were put on the roof. "The company issued little booklets," wrote the historian Henry Collins

In 1930, on the site of "Marble Row" on the east side of Fifth Avenue between Fifty-seventh and Fifty-eighth streets, a new and equally elegant row of commercial buildings was built: Cross & Cross were the architects of the fifteen-story New York Trust Building; just to the north was the Squibb Building, designed by Buchman & Kahn. Both buildings still stand.

Brown, "containing a directory of the fabled domiciles which were faithfully consulted by the passengers interested."

A new zoning law, permitting many more commercial structures on the avenue, passed in 1916. Taking advantage of the new zoning, the

The lobby of Buchman & Kahn's Squibb Building, entered through a handsome bronze portal, is decorated in an elegant and restrained art deco style. The central mural depicts Peter Minuit purchasing Manhattan from the Indians; on the ceiling was a map of Manhattan. The entrance and lobby remain, with some minor changes, and are scrupulously maintained.

Heckscher family put up a large office building in 1921 at 730 Fifth Avenue, on the southwest corner of Fifth Avenue and Fifty-seventh Street, where the house of Frederic Stevens had stood. Stevens, grandson of Albert Gallatin, U.S. secretary of the treasury and a banker himself (as well as a trustee of the New York Public Library and the Metropolitan Museum of Art), had built his house, known as 2 West

Fifty-seventh Street, in 1875–76. The Stevens house, designed by Warren & Wetmore, was considered highly "artistic," which in the vocabulary of the day meant that it was asymmetrical in its interiors and loaded with oversize Chinese vases, sixteenth-century tapestries, and stuffed birds (the entrance hall staircase had a full-size peacock perched on the banister). The finest room was the "Flemish ballroom," an eighteenth-century interior imported by the Stevenses from Belgium.

The new Heckscher building had interesting tenants in the early days. The Museum of Modern Art opened its first show there in November 1929 on an upper floor, and it was the first home (1923) of the *American Mercury* magazine, edited by George Jean Nathan and H. L. Mencken.

In 1924, a year after the Saks department store on Thirty-fourth Street merged with and was bought out by the Gimbel store, Horace Saks opened the Saks Fifth Avenue department store on Fifth Avenue at Forty-ninth to Fiftieth streets, offering many new attractions to shoppers. For instance, the Junior League maintained a bureau there to plan parties and order refreshments, entertainment, and even the proper guests, of which careful lists were kept. The Silhouette Shop offered massages, lotions, and electric blanket treatments "that, in a given time," according to one frank commentator, "miraculously adjust some very weird figures to fit Saks' clothes."

Equally elegant was the I. Miller shoe salon at 562 Fifth Avenue, which was done up inside "like suites of French drawing rooms." Tea was offered in the afternoon, usually with a Broadway star as hostess.

Close together on the east side of Fifth Avenue just below Fifty-seventh Street in the 1920s and 1930s were four great beauty salons: Dorothy Gray, Elizabeth Arden (number 691), Richard Hudnut, and Helena Rubinstein (number 715). Rubinstein once put up frames in her windows and had beautiful girls take turns posing in them in the manner of old masters, until the Fifth Avenue Association reminded her that the rules of the association forbade the use of living models in window displays. Most of these luxurious establishments specialized in the art of makeup, but several offered electrical massages and others new skin treatments. Rubinstein had a health-food restaurant, a health bar for fruit juices, and

The new St. Regis Hotel on the southeast corner of Fifth Avenue and Fifty-fifth Street, designed by Trowbridge & Livingston and completed in 1904, aroused the fury of its neighbors, who saw it as an encroachment of commerce into a residential neighborhood. It took an act of the New York state legislature, perhaps influenced by the vast interests of the hotel's builders, the Astor family, to overcome this resistance.

a tanning salon. A number of the most prominent hairdressers also had their establishments in the area.

The St. Regis Hotel, which has always used the address 2 East Fifty-fifth Street, on the southeast corner of Fifth Avenue, was built in 1904 by Trowbridge & Livingston, the architects of the B. Altman store. Nineteen stories contained 316 guest rooms. The builder was John Jacob Astor IV. The name was taken from St. Regis Lake in the Adirondacks, a favorite society resort and an exclusive one. The hotel was designed as the showpiece of the Astor hotel empire in New York. The St. Regis immediately became one of New York's, indeed the world's, grandest hotels. The management thought of their establishment as a "refuge for the richer class," offering the graces of a private townhouse without the worries of housekeeping.

The location of the St. Regis was its great attraction. It stood in the midst of a neighborhood that even in 1904 was still largely residential. Across Fifth Avenue was Vanderbilt Row. Nearby lived Whitneys, Huntingtons, and Rockefellers. The St. Regis made the point of its residential location in its publicity, telling prospective guests that the hotel was "withdrawn from the ordinary places of popular resort." In comparison to Fifth Avenue and Fifty-fifth Street, Thirty-fourth Street, where the Waldorf-Astoria stood, seemed commonplace, and the Times Square area, where the Astor Hotel stood, positively raffish.

Colonel Astor, as John Jacob Astor IV liked to be called (the rank derived from his Spanish–American War service), took a personal interest in the design of the St. Regis and had an opportunity to utilize his undeniable mechanical gifts. It was, for example, the first hotel in the world to be air-conditioned. Furthermore, each guest could regulate the temperature of his or her room, an astounding innovation and one that soon swept the hotel world.

The public rooms in the St. Regis were relatively small, a subtle indication that the management did not want the crowds that milled in Peacock Alley at the Waldorf-Astoria or in the vast lobby of the Astor in Times Square. No conventioneers should apply for rooms. The public areas were sumptuously decorated. Ava Willing Astor, Colonel Astor's wife, took a personal interest in the decorating. She was responsible for the dining room, called the Salle Cathay, dripping with antique *chinoiserie*. On the Fifth Avenue side was an outdoor terrace where one could have refreshments, lost when Fifth Avenue was widened. In the Men's Bar hung the painting of *Old King Cole* by Maxfield Parrish, formerly in the Knickerbocker Hotel, another Astor establishment. Society quickly adopted the St. Regis. When the old Waldorf-Astoria Hotel closed, Albert Bagby transferred his celebrated Musical Mornings to the St. Regis, a sure sign of acceptance. During the nightclub years of the 1930s the St. Regis had many clubs, attracting for the most part, a rather conservative, and very well-heeled crowd. Joseph Urban, the flamboyant architect, designed the Seaglades nightclub, where Vincent Lopez's orchestra played. During the summer they played for dancing in the Japanese-style roof garden of the hotel.

The two hundred buildings on twelve rather seedy acres bounded by West Forty-eighth and Fifty-first streets between Fifth and Sixth avenues were mostly solid brownstones that by the 1920s had seen better days. Many were rooming houses, some had degenerated into tenements, and an astonishing number concealed speakeasies on their ground floors. The land beneath them, where Dr. Hosack had grown his beneficial plants, was owned by Columbia University. The neighborhood was generally known as Manhattan Square and was considered ripe for new development.

John D. Rockefeller, Jr., lived just north of the square on West Fifty-fourth Street. He and his father seem to have avoided Fifth Avenue, the natural habitat for millionaires but with connotations of fashion and even frivolity, which the sober Rockefellers abhorred. In 1929 the Rockefellers leased the land under Manhattan Square from Columbia, first planning to build a new opera house and some office buildings.

Slowly, their plans for the plot became grandiose, and soon the Rockefeller interests, despite the Depression, were building Rockefeller Center, a vast complex of office buildings, shops, and theaters generally believed to be the largest architectural project ever undertaken by private enterprise.

The centerpiece and tallest structure, the seventy-story RCA Building, was completed in 1933. In terms of floor space it was the largest office building in the world. Radio City Music Hall, then and still the largest indoor theater in the world, seating 6,200, opened its first show on 27 December 1932. Office buildings for Time and Life, the Associated Press, Eastern Airlines, and U.S. Rubber followed in the first wave of construction, which was completed in 1940.

Originally conceived as the site of a new Metropolitan Opera House, the 17 acres bounded by Fifth and Sixth Avenues and Forty-eighth and Fifty-first streets were developed by John D. Rockefeller, Jr., between 1931 and 1940 to create Rockefeller Center. (The complex was designed by three firms: L. A. Reinhard and Henry Hofmeister; Harvey Wiley Corbett, Wallace K. Harrison, and William H. McMurray; and Raymond Hood and Jacques André Fouilhoux.) Like the Flatiron Building, Rockefeller Center was embraced by New Yorkers only gradually.

The principal tenants along Sixth Avenue, the western terminus of the earliest construction, were RKO (Radio-Keith-Orpheum) and the National Broadcasting Company, communications giants; along with the Music Hall, the whole section was called Radio City.

The Fifth Avenue side was reserved for international buildings and elegant shops with a seasonally planted channel that subtly led the visitor into the heart of the complex. A statue of Prometheus (immediately called the golden boy by those not too familiar with Greek myths) by Paul Manship has overlooked the central plaza since 1934.

In 1947, as soon as the end of World War II released construction materials, building began again to the west, bringing Rockefeller Center almost to Times Square.

The Rockefeller Center buildings along Sixth Avenue were intended for the entertainment industry, and included the RCA Building (pictured), the RKO Building, and Radio City Music Hall. The buildings along Fifth Avenue were international agencies and included the British Empire Building, the Maison Française, and the Palazzo d'Italia. Private gardens were on the roofs.

6

The Silk
Purse

Fifty-ninth Street to 110th Street

•

While Fifth Avenue below Fifty-ninth Street was filling up in stages with brownstone houses, churches, hotels, and shops, the northern part of New York remained in its natural state. The beauty of Manhattan Island is manmade: beneath the stone and brick lies a surface not naturally attractive—stony and waterlogged. The area above Fifty-ninth Street was particularly featureless, flat, and uninteresting. On the east side it was almost entirely undeveloped between Fifth Avenue and the East River, and there were only straggling developments west from Fifth Avenue to the Hudson River. Streets had been laid out on paper on the grid plan of 1811, but neither graded nor paved, so the area was practically without visible landmarks as well as largely uninhabited.

Edgar Allan Poe, when a free-lance journalist in New York, was one of the few writers who tried to find interest in this unpromising landscape. He wrote in 1844 that while "roaming far and wide over this island of Mannahatta [it was a literary affectation of the time to use the Indian name]," he had discovered that "some portions of its interior have a certain air of rocky sterility which may impress some imaginations as simply dreary—to me it conveys the sublime. Trees are few; but some of the shrubbery is exceedingly picturesque. No less so are the prevalent shanties of the Irish squatters."

It was then customary to blame most social ills on the Irish immigrants flooding into the city, but the squatters were not all Irish; blacks and American Indians and other races also lived in shanties that clustered on the west side of the path that became Central Park West. Estimates of the number of squatters varied wildly: contemporaries were convinced there were thousands; modern estimates run around fifteen hundred. When work on Central Park began in 1857, about two hundred makeshift houses were counted. Some of the inhabitants gathered rags and bones for sale, some raised goats and pigs; according to police, petty thievery was the occupation of many.

Egbert Viele, chief engineer for Central Park, summed up the area in 1855:

> It was for the most part a succession of stone quarries, interspersed with pestiferous swamps. The entire ground was the refuge of about five thousand [sic] squatters, dwelling in rude huts of their own construction, and living off the refuse of the city.... Horses, cows, swine, goats, cats, geese, and chickens swarmed everywhere, destroying what little verdure they found. Even the roots in the ground were exterminated until the rocks were laid bare, giving an air of utter desolation to the scene....

Frederick Law Olmsted, after being appointed superintendent of the park, said in disgust: "I had not been aware that the park was such a very nasty place. In fact, the low grounds were steeped in the overflow of the pigsties, slaughter houses, and bone-boiling works, and the stench was sickening."

Livestock in the area above Fifty-ninth Street was a continuing problem. Stray and unwanted animals appear to have been dumped in the area, where they bred in astonishing numbers. Mongrel dogs threatened walkers; some alarmed observers claimed that there were over a hundred thousand of them, which is unlikely but there were enough to be a problem. Goats, cattle, and horses roamed freely. Some of the animals were slaughtered by the squatters and boiled down for their bones. The entire area was one of the city's numerous hazards to health and aesthetics. It was astonishing that a city as aggressive and advanced as New York would so long tolerate such an appalling wilderness only a few miles to the north of its bustling center.

One of the first permanent constructions in the area actually took advantage of its remoteness and unattractiveness. The state of New York built an arsenal there in 1848, when the war with Mexico had put everybody's mind on military affairs. The location was on Fifth Avenue at East Sixty-fourth Street, four miles from City Hall, a safety measure since highly explosive arms and ammunition were stored in the little brick building. Six years later the Arsenal, the address of which is 821 Fifth Avenue, became the property of the city, which left it there, without the armaments, when Central Park was built. For years it was the city's museum of natural history. Later it became, and remains, the headquarters of the New York City Department of Parks and Recreation.

Until the middle of the nineteenth century, between East Sixty-sixth and Sixty-eighth streets along Fifth Avenue and east to Third Avenue was Hamilton Square, a little public park designed to break up the grid system of streets in the neighborhood and to afford a much-needed open area, the same purpose, in fact, that Central Park was to serve. In 1807, when still the property of the Corporation of the City of New York (that is, of the city itself in its capacity to own property, among other functions no longer in operation), the area was described as "the most elevated of any land on this island south of Harlem [which] commands a superb view of the East River, and the variegated landscape in the vicinity of Hellgate [the narrow strait that connects the East River and Long Island Sound]." Twenty-six lots around the square were offered for sale with the stipulation that the purchasers should maintain the square.

There was no egalitarian nonsense about the offer, which stated plainly, "In addition to every other circumstance, the lots have been designedly laid out to attract a genteel neighborhood, whose wealth and taste will

THE PLAZA HOTELS, from CENTRAL PARK

undoubtedly embellish this high favored spot, universally acknowledged
to be the first on this island." It is possible to see in this blunt statement
the future exclusivity of the Upper East Side, but very few well-to-do
citizens heeded the call; Hamilton Square was much too far from the
settled parts of the city to attract residents.

Hamilton Square, like other promises of city government, had a short existence. When construction of Central Park began, the city government
decided there was no need for two parks so close together, so in 1869, the
square was closed and the streets demarcating it driven through to the
East River.

In the pattern of civic betterment in New York, Central Park existed
as an ideal and a topic for debate for decades before anyone got around
to doing anything about it. The obvious need to clean up the area, the
pressure of building from the southern part of the city, and the urgings of

During the nineteenth century, the largest and best hotels, including the Fifth Avenue Hotel and the Waldorf-Astoria, were already found on Fifth Avenue. By the early 1930s, Fifth Avenue around its intersection with Fifty-ninth Street and Grand Army Plaza, was lined with some of the most renowned hotels in the world, including the Pierre (far left), the Sherry-Netherland (with spire), the Savoy-Plaza (with two chimneys), now the site of the General Motors building, and the Plaza (with dormers).

notable New Yorkers such as William Cullen Bryant and Washington Irving finally roused the lethargic city government. Once it was agreed that there was to be a park, the pace became astonishingly fast: the land was purchased in 1856; in 1857 Frederick Law Olmsted and Calvert Vaux were chosen, after a competition, to design the park and construction began; and the park was opened to the public in 1859. A schedule like that for one of the largest and most important public projects ever carried out in New York City is astounding and enviable in the twentieth century, when public works can easily take decades. The northern boundary of the park was originally 106th Street, then 110th Street, as it is today; the final tract contains 840 acres and measures two and a half miles long by half a mile wide.

The Croton Aqueduct, furnishing the city with clean and plentiful water, and Central Park, supplying space and air, were amenities that enabled New York City to rank with London and Paris. The comparison delighted civic-minded New Yorkers. The two great projects were even combined: the receiving reservoir for Croton water was located in the park between Eighty-sixth and Ninety-sixth streets.

Central Park with its extraordinary combination of the bucolic and the urban, with its paths that seemed remote although in sight of buildings, was instantly popular and became, in the words of Sigmund Romberg in his musical *Up in Central Park,* "the big backyard of the city." By 1865 the park was receiving more than seven million visitors a year.

The carefully planned rusticity of Olmsted and Vaux came under attack almost immediately by intrusions in the form of playing fields, statuary, and theaters, beginning a battle between preservers and ornamenters that has lasted nearly a century and a half. Among the more insane proposals have been a full-scale replication of the World War I trenches of Verdun, a ceaseless people mover, and a two-mile-long racetrack. About ten thousand statues have also been proposed.

The battle to maintain a countrified and peaceful landscape was hard fought. Olmsted and Vaux provided a dairy where milk drinks were served, and sheep were grazed in the southern portion of the park between Sixty-sixth and Sixty-ninth streets in an area still known as Sheep

Meadow. High-class animals like the sheep were introduced, no doubt, to dispel the image of the mangy strays that formerly infested the park area. Until 1934, when sheep were banished and the only animals residing in the park were those in the zoo behind the Arsenal, their sheepfold was the building that has become the restaurant Tavern on the Green. The sheep were available for purchase, and their mutton was esteemed by gourmets, probably because of the superior grazing on the cultivated park grass. In 1879 the gastronome Samuel Ward, noted for the selectivity of his dinners—he called a menu "the plan of campaign"—served *selle d'agneau de Central Park* with mint sauce, *petits pois*, tomatoes, and potato croquettes accompanied by Moët et Chandon Grand Crémant poured from "imperial magnums."

Central Park was for half a century the preserve and showplace of the horse and horse-drawn vehicle. Every afternoon from three o'clock to six, fine equipages drawn by well-groomed horses drove slowly through the park, "the procession of wealth, beauty and fashion in Central Park," as newspapers delighted in calling the scene. Ten years after the park was opened, Walt Whitman went there to observe: "Ten thousand vehicles careering through the Park this perfect afternoon. Such a show! and I have seen all—watch'd it narrowly, and at my leisure. Private barouches, cabs and coupés, some fine horseflesh—lapdogs, footmen, fashions, foreigners, cockades on hats, crests on panels—the full oceanic tide of New York's wealth and 'gentility.'" From his experience he drew the unfounded but entirely Whitmanesque conclusion that unlike the workmen of "good general physique" and "clear eyes," the rich in America were "far from happy."

At the very end of the nineteenth century, automobiles were occasionally seen on New York City streets, but not in Central Park. Motorists were forbidden to enter the park, a rule that chagrined the owners of expensive new motorcars. The park's management maintained that motors would scare the horses, a trite excuse. After a series of tests in 1899 showed horses took the appearance of automobiles stoically ("unmoved," the *New York Times* said), special permits were issued for automobiles to enter the park; before long even the permits were abolished. Traffic was

Prominent Fifth Avenue architect Richard Morris Hunt was hired to design an entrance facade to provide some unity to the agglomeration of buildings that comprised the Metropolitan Museum of Art since the completion in 1880 of the original building by Calvert Vaux. Hunt died during the construction of his Renaissance Revival addition, begun in 1895 and completed by Hunt's son, Richard Howland Hunt, in 1902. In recent years the building has seen extensive additions into Central Park at its north, south, and west.

soon considerable, and the struggle began to keep the park as much as possible a pedestrian preserve; a hundred years later it continues.

One of the earliest intrusions into the park was the Metropolitan Museum of Art. The site above Seventy-ninth Street was chosen in 1872. Calvert Vaux, one of the designers of Central Park, and Jacob Wrey Mould, one of the less distinguished architects of the time, collaborated on a small permanent building in neo-Gothic style on the east side of the park, which opened to the public on 30 March 1880. In 1888 the southwest wing in the neo-Grec style was added by Theodore Weston. The building then faced south; had it remained that way it would have been the focus of a noble vista looking up Fifth Avenue, but instead, the entire museum was reoriented east toward Fifth Avenue. The Vaux and Mould building is now concealed by later accretions in a bewildering variety of architectural styles and by the incorporation of parts of two older buildings. The central Fifth Avenue section designed by Richard Morris Hunt and his son, Richard Howland Hunt, in the neo-Roman style was opened in 1902, the first of many changes designed to give majesty to the building. McKim, Mead & White tinkered with the building in 1906; then there was a long period of architectural peace until the 1960s when a vast program of expansion began. Now, like most of the great museums of the world, the Metropolitan is a hodge-podge of styles and can be very

confusing visually. Between the 1960s and the 1980s numerous reconstructions were made by Kevin Roche John Dinkeloo & Associates.

Ten blocks down the street was the Lenox Library, which opened at about the same time as the Metropolitan Museum of Art. James Lenox was still accumulating books in his house on Fifth Avenue and Twelfth Street, but he was overwhelmed by his collection, which included, for example, four thousand editions of the Bible, and gave it to the public, at least in theory. He had Richard Morris Hunt build a stately home for the library along Fifth Avenue on the entire blockfront between Seventieth and Seventy-first streets on Lenox Hill, once farm property that had been owned by his father. The library, which opened in 1877, was not a friendly neighborhood institution. Age (he was nearly eighty) had not made Lenox

In 1877, James Lenox moved his massive book collection from his town house on Fifth Avenue and West Twelfth Street to this mausoleum-like structure on the east side of Fifth Avenue between Seventieth and Seventy-first streets. Designed by Richard Morris Hunt, the Lenox Library was built on a site that was once a farm owned by the Lenox family. The Frick Collection now occupies the site.

any less protective of his books, and the reading public complained bitterly that the library admitted almost no one and that, once within, you were expected to view, not use, the books and manuscripts. It closed for most of the summer and did not install electric lights until 1894. The *New York Herald* said nastily, "The Lenox Library seems to be conducted on the principle of doing the least good to the least number"; and *Life* magazine ran a cartoon showing cannons on the top of the building to ward off visitors. In 1895 it was consolidated with the Astor and Tilden collections to become the New York Public Library. After tedious and lengthy negotiations with the Pittsburgh steel magnate Henry Clay Frick the Lenox trustees sold their building to Frick, who had it demolished and commissioned the architects Carrère & Hastings, who had designed the New York Public Library, to build him a marble palace. In 1935, after architectural modification by John Russell Pope, it became a public institution. Demolition was the fate of most of Hunt's many buildings in New York. As if to make up for the destruction of his work, an elaborate memorial to Hunt with a statue of him by Daniel Chester French was erected in 1898 opposite the Frick Collection.

The completion of Central Park would, it seems, have immediately opened the area to the east for residential development. In fact, there was a gap of decades before the fifty-one blocks between Fifty-ninth and 110th streets filled with buildings; there was no residence north of Seventy-ninth Street, for example, until 1876 and few buildings of any sort. The price of lots rose steadily. The attraction of a house facing the park was obvious, and no one doubted that the neighborhood had a future, but those who could afford to live there stubbornly remained in their brownstones below the park until the inevitable advance of commerce finally drove them north of Fifty-ninth Street.

The wall of lavish private houses on Fifth Avenue facing Central Park was not a Gilded Age phenomenon. The novels set in Fifth Avenue houses in the 1870s and 1880s—Edith Wharton's *The Age of Innocence*, for example—describe houses below Fifty-ninth Street. Active construction on Fifth Avenue really began in the 1880s and lasted until about 1914. Perhaps the most important single date is 1895, when Richard Morris Hunt completed his great chateau for Mrs. William B. Astor and her son

John Jacob on the northeast corner of Fifth Avenue and Sixty-fifth Street. Where the Astors led, others would soon follow. Nevertheless, vacant lots dotted Fifth Avenue well into the twentieth century. Some lots never had a private house at all; the first building was an apartment house. In all, there were about one hundred private houses built on Fifth Avenue between Fifty-ninth and Ninety-sixth streets.

The double house built in 1895 by Richard Morris Hunt on the northeast corner of Fifth Avenue and Sixty-fifth Street for Mrs. William B. Astor and her son, John Jacob, *and his family, contained separate residences linked by grand first-floor rooms for entertaining.*

The art gallery of the Astor house shows the opulence favored by wealthy New Yorkers during the late nineteenth century. The gallery, situated in the center of the house, was used for the Astors' frequent receptions and balls. Architect Hunt had a penchant for ceilings heavily embellished with nearly life-size statuary, producing an impressive if somewhat top-heavy effect.

The northern stretches of the avenue remained largely vacant, and land was much cheaper than it was twenty or thirty blocks to the south. Mount Sinai Hospital, opened in 1855 as Jews' Hospital in the City of New York, was able to buy ample land in 1898 to put up ten hospital buildings with 456 beds. More houses were put up on the side streets. The Upper East Side above Fifty-ninth Street, or at least a narrow strip of it extending from

Central Park just across Madison Avenue to Fourth Avenue (later Park Avenue), was already known as an expensive neighborhood of town houses with rich, successful, and occasionally extravagant inhabitants. Their doings, especially the more frivolous, fascinated newspapers in the way the scandals of movie stars do now. In one of Edgar Saltus's tepid New York "society" novels written around 1900, the bored hero, whose only occupation is the occasional trip to Wall Street to clip coupons from his bonds, lives in his own house in the high East Sixties. He is terribly weary of the world and his surroundings: "What irked him most was his durance in the precinct in which he lived, and which, with Central Park on one side, Madison Avenue on the other, Seventy-second street for frontier, and the Plaza for approach, is colloquially known as 'Vanity Square.'"

The Upper East Side and Upper Fifth Avenue, when building finally began there, had some of the same family neighborhood quality that Lower Fifth Avenue had: members of well-known New York families clustered within a few blocks. The Arnold and Constable families, owners of the well-known Fifth Avenue dry-goods store, were major property owners on Upper Fifth Avenue soon after Central Park opened, buying ten lots on East Eighty-first Street as early as 1866. Aaron Arnold, the English-born founder of the store, came to the United States in 1823. James Mansell Constable, also English-born, worked for Arnold, married his daughter, and became a partner in the firm. Aaron's son, Richard Arnold, was a real-estate speculator who built brownstones on East Eighty-first Street off Fifth, several of which still exist. He himself lived in a large house on the northeast corner of Fifth Avenue and Eighty-third Street until his death in 1886. When built in 1878–79, it was the only house in the block facing Fifth Avenue. It was demolished to make way for an apartment building in 1914–15. Other Arnolds and Constables, related in several ways, lived and owned lots in the neighborhood. In 1897 the *New York Herald-Tribune* listed the family as the fifth largest landowners in New York City.

The Brokaw family entrenched itself on Fifth Avenue around Seventy-ninth Street. In 1887–88, Isaac V. Brokaw, head of Brokaw Brothers, clothing manufacturers, built an imposing home in the French

Renaissance, or François I, style at 1 East Seventy-ninth Street. It abounded in turrets and gables and had an especially striking sunken entryway at front so deep it resembled a moat. In 1905–07 he built twin houses in the same style at 984 and 985 Fifth Avenue for two of his sons, and in 1914 a house at 5–7 East Seventy-ninth Street for his daughter. The entire complex was demolished in 1965–68, despite the outrage of preservationists and architectural historians.

The François I architecture of the Brokaw house was the most popular on Fifth Avenue when the great houses went up; its everyday name was the Fifth Avenue style. The rich in the United States had a rather uninformed but touching admiration for Renaissance France, no doubt the influence of the École des Beaux-Arts, where Richard Morris Hunt, society's favorite architect, had studied. Both the Vanderbilts and the Astors commissioned French Renaissance palaces on Fifth Avenue from him. Admiration extended to imitation not only in houses but in fancy dress: at the great costume parties of the era—the Vanderbilt ball, the Bradley Martin ball, and the James Hazen Hyde ball—the rooms swarmed with ladies dressed (but decently) as Diane de Poitiers and gentlemen masquerading as the Duc de Guise. One fancies the revelers would have been hard put to explain the complicated intrigues of the Valois dynasty, but the costumes were spectacular and extremely costly.

Across Seventy-ninth Street from the Brokaw family enclave was the even more ornate French Gothic house built in 1897–99 by C. P. H. Gilbert for Isaac D. Fletcher, president of the New York Coal Tar Company. Fletcher, a major art collector, left most of his estate to the Metropolitan Museum of Art, which he could see from his house on the southeast corner of Seventy-ninth Street. The long portion of the still-standing house is on the side street, and the address has always been 2 East Seventy-ninth Street. The five-story house is covered with very rich ornamentation, including enchanting seahorses and other marine creatures. After Fletcher died in 1917, his house was sold to Harry F. Sinclair of the Sinclair Oil Company. During the 1922 scandal of the Teapot Dome oil reserves he was deeply involved and served a prison term for contempt of court. That episode does not seem to have impeded his business career as he was later chairman of the Richfield Oil Company as well as owner of the St. Louis Browns baseball team.

Sinclair sold the house in 1930 for four hundred fifty thousand dollars to surprising buyers: Augustus van Horne Stuyvesant and his sister Ann, who were then in their sixties. They were descendants of Governor Peter Stuyvesant; in fact, Augustus was the last male in the direct line. They were very rich from real-estate holdings in the city, especially in the area of Second Avenue below Fourteenth Street, holdings that had originally been Governor Stuyvesant's. Since both were shy and unsociable, their reasons for moving into such a huge house in the middle of the new rich so late in their lives are obscure, except that their lives had been spent on Fifth Avenue: born on Twentieth and Fifth, growing up at Twenty-first and Fifth, and then living at 3 East Fifty-seventh, one door off Fifth. Ann died in 1938, and Augustus, a bachelor, became reclusive, confining his outdoor activities to a short daily constitutional in the neighborhood. For years he attended the Stuyvesant church at East Tenth Street and Second Avenue, St. Marks in the Bowery, every fifth Sunday (he was demonstrating his displeasure with the rector, with whom he had quarreled) being conveyed there in his Rolls-Royce. While there, he inspected the Stuyvesant vault, where eighty or ninety of his relatives were buried. Otherwise, his butler once said, "All Mr. Stuyvesant does is sit in front of a picture of Franklin D. Roosevelt and cuss." When he died in 1953 at the age of eighty-three, he was buried in the Stuyvesant vault, and since he was the last male Stuyvesant, the vault was sealed. Augustus's entire estate and that of his sisters went to St. Luke's Hospital. Two years later their house became the headquarters of the Ukrainian Institute of America.

An early and unusually large house was built in 1881–83 by Robert L. Stuart and his wife, who like so many New Yorkers of their class, had moved uptown from Fifth Avenue and East Twentieth Street. He was the son of a successful candy manufacturer who entered sugar refining, the origin of many New York City fortunes. His wife was Mary McCrea, daughter of a merchant and well-to-do in her own right. The new house extended 55 feet along Fifth Avenue and 136 feet along Sixty-eighth Street. It had to be large to hold the Stuarts' possessions: they owned a huge collection of nearly 250 paintings along with engravings, natural history specimens, and archaeological artifacts. They were notable in their time for patronizing American artists, such as Eastman Johnson and William Sidney Mount, although they also owned the usual contemporary French Salon paintings, beloved by American millionaires. The Stuarts were very charitable. On the death of Mrs. Stuart in 1891, after only a few years in her great house, the New York Public Library inherited, probably with mixed feelings, not only the notable library but also the collections of minerals, fossils, and archaeological shards, with the awkward restriction that none of the Stuart collections could ever be exhibited to the public on Sundays.

A few eccentrics built far up the avenue: in 1883, Jacob Ruppert, a brewer whose beer was popular with New Yorkers for generations, built a house on the southeast corner of Ninety-third Street. His only near neighbor was the New-York Magdalen Asylum, formerly known as the New-York Female Moral Reform Society, a refuge for former prostitutes, on East Eighty-eighth Street. The decoration of some rooms in Ruppert's house reflected his Germanic heritage—his father came from Bavaria in 1830—heavy carvings with musical motifs abounding, a medieval musicians' gallery in the dining room, and embossed leather on the walls; other rooms were in the lighter and increasingly popular Louis XVI style.

Countess Annie Leary, one of the stalwart figures of New York society for decades, lived and entertained at 1032 Fifth Avenue, just above Eighty-fourth Street. Her father, James Leary, had made, unlikely as it seems, a fortune selling beaver hats at a shop in the old Astor House Hotel on the corner of Broadway and Vesey. Presumably, he had also invested in real estate, because he was rich enough to install his wife and six children at the fashionable address 90 Fifth Avenue. One of the very few Roman Catholic and Irish families to be accepted in New York society, which was still staunchly Dutch Reform and Episcopalian in religion, the Learys, especially Annie, were famous for their donations to their church. Annie was a papal countess for her benefactions, which included the Arthur Leary Memorial Chapel in the courtyard of the old Bellevue Hospital. She insisted on being addressed as countess and in her Fifth Avenue house the crimson portieres were embroidered with her papal coronet.

Her Fifth Avenue house—she also had one in Newport—was arranged for entertaining, with no fewer than sixty-eight enormous mirrors, for which the countess had a special fondness. She was perhaps most notable for being the only friend of the famous miser and stock market operator Hettie Green, known as the Witch of Wall Street. The countess was responsible for rescuing Hettie's daughter Sylvia from the boarding-house in Hoboken where her mother insisted on living—and cooking on a gas ring—and arranging for her debut. Her entertaining and her charities cost her dearly: she left a very small estate when she died in 1919 and was buried in Old St. Patrick's Church on Mott Street.

Externally, the French styles gave a certain uniformity to Upper Fifth Avenue; internally, the houses built from the 1880s to the end of the century also had a certain uniformity of decor. Interchangeable rooms probably reflected the artistic uneasiness of the new rich; there were many on the avenue. When unfamiliar with decorating, one was safer to copy the neighbors. The massive compilation of photographs of contemporary American interiors called *Artistic Houses*, issued in 1883–84, illustrates many rooms in Fifth Avenue houses. They are remarkably alike. Almost without exception they seem airless and crammed with the Victorian clutter that evokes such horror in the late twentieth-century mind.

Walls were paneled in most of the reception rooms—the "public rooms" of the house—the drawing room, library, and dining room, usually with the dark woods mahogany, ebony, and teak. The paneling was sometimes imported as whole rooms from Europe. Not simply wood-covered walls, the paneling was broken up, usually into three parts: wainscoting below; a central panel of wallpaper, fabric, or embossed leather; and above, some sort of decorated frieze (a procession of children in classical or medieval dress or bacchantes in not-too-revealing costumes was typical). Ceilings were beamed or carved or painted; not infrequently all three techniques were used. Walls were also hung with paintings, mirrors, and tapestries or other textiles; and there were plate rails for the display of china.

Heavy curtains, often in two or three layers, kept out the natural light, since they were usually closed or tied back only a short way. Lambrequins, the short drapery at the top of the curtains, "which collected the dust that drifted in from the street," as one memoirist remembered, decorated every window. Window shades were green, and it was customary to have them drawn exactly halfway down the windows (all the way down if someone in the house had died). For this there was a good reason: the houses, however palatial, were town houses with only a small area between the drawing room and the street, offering little privacy. Doors within the house were hung, too, with portieres, heavy curtains that fell to the floor, much beloved by the era. "Persian" rugs were sometimes hung as portieres, as were tapestries or Oriental robes cut and hemmed for the purpose. Portieres were originally to retain warmth in drafty houses but, after the advent of central heating, became merely decorative and useful in separating rooms for privacy. Persian rugs deadened the sound in rooms, as did numerous pillows, throws, and shawls on every sofa and tapestries on the walls. The craze for "Moorish" rooms, which no Berber could recognize, brought even more cushions and rugs—along with little tables inlaid with mother-of-pearl, water pipes, and even scimitars—into already suffocating spaces.

It was the era of bric-a-brac. Ceramics, especially, were widely appreciated and collected. "Chinamania" was a recognized social pursuit; young men and women formed china-collecting clubs and toured rural antique shops on their bicycles. But china, displayed in nearly every room in the house, was only the beginning of the clutter: vases filled with peacock feathers, small bronzes, clocks, incense burners, and stuffed birds had their place. Most of these possessions were not the accumulation of a lifetime or inheritance, but souvenirs of foreign travel. Rich Americans already had a well-merited reputation abroad as champion shoppers. Small wonder that contemporary letters and journals say so much about "the baggage" and its transportation. Twenty or thirty trunks, and those large, were not at all unusual on the homeward voyage. Some ornaments were supplied by dealers in bric-a-brac, who were just coming into their own in New York and importing shiploads. Virtually everything was of foreign origin: European, Middle Eastern, Asian, probably in that order. Although a fair number of the Fifth Avenue families—the Hamilton Fishes, for example—were of long American ancestry, few, if any, showed off heirloom furniture and paintings in their parlors; Windsor chairs and Copley portraits were thin on the ground.

Most objects were vaguely labeled "antique," or simply "old," without being very specific as to age. Neither was the nation of origin very important.

William C. Whitney commissioned his friend Stanford White to renovate the house on the northeast corner of Fifth Avenue and Sixty-eighth Street that he bought for his second wife in 1896. White concentrated on the house's interior, spending over one million dollars over three years. The result was an ornate scheme typical of late-nineteenth-century New York, as seen in this 1899 photograph of the drawing room.

Elbridge T. Gerry was one of the most distinguished New Yorkers of his time: a prominent lawyer, he founded the Society for the Prevention of Cruelty to Children and served twice as commodore of the New York Yacht Club. Gerry died in 1927, and that same year his imposing house on the southeast corner of Fifth Avenue and Sixty-first Street was demolished. Two years later the renowned Pierre Hotel was built on the site.

Labeling objects in curatorial fashion with place and period is a twentieth-century style. Reproductions of old objects were mingled with the genuine antique without anyone being the wiser. To say one owned only a reproduction of a celebrated object brought forth no sneer, as it might today; "exact copy" was not a derogatory expression. Furniture, in particular, was as likely to be reproduction as period. American impatience played a great role: it was quite common for owners to have furniture made in a certain style, say Louis XIII, when a period piece could not be found quickly. Some of these reproductions, mostly made to order in Paris, were of very high quality and quite as costly as originals. They were in better condition, which appealed to American collectors, never really accustomed to the threadbare antiques accepted by Europeans.

Descriptions of the new Fifth Avenue houses and their interiors reveled in the word *rare,* an adjective grossly overused in talking about art. *Priceless,* too, was popular, certainly inapplicable since the owners had nearly always bought the objects themselves. It was an age of exegesis: works of art called forth more words than sensations, and the highest compliment paid to an object was to describe what it depicted and its association, however farfetched, with, say, Catherine de' Medicis. The idea that works of art speak for themselves did not seem to occur to anyone.

Residents of Fifth Avenue were great buyers of pictures: collections, by twentieth-century standards, were huge—two hundred paintings hanging in a house was not unusual. The most popular paintings, those exhibited at the Paris Salon, the huge art show held each year in Paris, lent themselves especially to explanation and discussion; they were "storytelling pictures," which meant that the proud owner could point out the narrative to visitors, along with the painting's supposed fidelity to history or nature without being called upon for an artistic judgment. Collis P. Huntington claimed to sit for hours in the art gallery of his Fifth Avenue house gazing at a storyteller he owned by Vibert called *The Missionary's Return,* in which a ragged priest is recounting his adventures to a fat, stay-at-home cardinal. The highest-paid painter in the world at the time was Jean-Louis-Ernest Meissonier, whose stiff reconstructions of Napoleonic battles were eagerly bought by American collectors like the Vanderbilts. His work epitomized this storytelling taste, and Fifth Avenue houses were loaded with Meissoniers.

Although in photographs these rooms seem higgledy-piggledy to modern eyes, the occupants spent much time and thought on carefully arranging their possessions. It seemed important to have as many pieces of furniture as possible. The excessive number of tables was partly accounted for by their value as spaces for display. Hardly anything was built in: instead of shelving for the library, owners preferred to buy a series of freestanding bookcases, often unmatching, and line them up along the walls, the tops displaying cloisonné vases and stuffed birds. Most rooms were not confined as to period or culture, although there were "Japanese" and "Moorish" rooms, too.

The Fifth Avenue houses of rich New Yorkers were large, but many of them had the limitations imposed by the New York street plan. Lots were narrow and long; consequently rooms, too, were narrow, and those in the back had neither view nor light. Ceilings, however, were generally high, eighteen feet or more, and their height accounts for the elaborate wall treatments. One reason so many rooms appeared crowded was that many of the numerous objects brought back from Europe—tapestries, for example—had been designed for castles and palaces and really were too large for New York townhouses.

Late in the century a thinning out of decor began, although rooms were far from empty and some clung to their portieres and stuffed peacocks. At the same time a new wave of house building began.

When Jay Gould died in 1892, leaving an estate officially appraised at $73,224,547.08, a figure generally thought to be about half the true value, his son George Gould assumed management of the railroads and telegraph companies that were the major part of the Gould fortune. He and his wife, Edith Kingdon, gave up their relatively modest house at 1 East Forty-seventh, possibly to get away from his bossy sister Helen, who presided over Jay's nearby house at 579 Fifth Avenue, and built a new home at 857 Fifth Avenue, at the northeast corner of Sixty-seventh Street. The new house was next door to the house of financier Thomas Fortune Ryan, an immense house of fifty rooms, including gold-and-white reception rooms and a "Moorish" drawing room with mother-of-pearl wainscoting and the skins of tigers and polar bears (neither found in Moorish lands) on the floor.

George Gould owned other Fifth Avenue property. In 1910, when his daughter Marjorie Gould married Anthony J. Drexel, Jr., of the

Mrs. George Gould acted on the New York stage as Edith Kingdon, retiring in 1886 when she married the eldest son of Jay Gould. The George Goulds moved to this house on the northeast corner of Fifth Avenue and Sixty-seventh Street when their house on Forty-seventh Street proved too small for their social ambitions. In 1906, they engaged society architect Horace Trumbauer to build a classical marble mansion that would accommodate their opulent lifestyle.

Philadelphia banking family, George gave her 1015 Fifth Avenue in the block between East Eighty-second and East Eighty-third streets; at the time only one other lot in that block had a house on it.

A few years later, in 1899, Howard Gould, another son of Jay, paid the incredible sum of $450,000 for a lot on Fifth Avenue above East Seventy-second Street measuring 77 by 130 feet, when he also married an actress, Katherine Clemmons. They were at odds almost from the beginning of their marriage. When they were divorced in 1909, she got the house in the divorce settlement, but Howard, in a skillful maneuver worthy of his father, arranged a foreclosure by his brother George and got the house back. Katherine became a fairly successful novelist. Howard made a great deal more money than he had inherited and, when he died in 1959, left $62 million to twenty-eight heirs, mostly Goulds, but because he had neglected taking the most elementary tax protections, taxes amounted to no less than $50 million. Another Gould brother, Edwin, built a house at number 936, on the southeast corner of Seventy-fifth Street.

Although the stretch of Fifth Avenue between East Fifty-ninth and East 110th was by no means entirely built up, there was considerable trade in houses. Adolph Lewisohn, the German-American financier, for instance, lived early in the twentieth century at number 881 in a brownstone in the center of the block between East Sixty-ninth and Seventieth streets. His house had two entrances on Fifth Avenue, one through the basement, which led to a room that Lewisohn "uses largely in connection with the various philanthropical enterprises in which he is engaged," commented *Town & Country* magazine in 1917. Among other benefactions, he donated the money for the building of Lewisohn Stadium, seating six thousand people, at City College of New York, dedicated in 1915 (and demolished in 1973). The Lewisohn house had formerly belonged to Heber R. Bishop, a rich westerner and indefatigable host, and had a huge ballroom which, "with its elaborate decorations in ivory and antique gold," the same magazine remarked, "is of the Louis XV period and resembles the mirrored galleries in the great rooms at Versailles." Bishop owned a collection of Oriental jade; when he gave it to the Metropolitan Museum of Art, he had his ballroom reproduced as a background for the collection.

Another family enclave developed around East Seventy-ninth Street, that of the Woolworths, the five-and-ten dynasty. The patriarch of the family, Franklin W. Woolworth, built his own house first at 990 Fifth Avenue in 1899, on the northeast corner of Eightieth Street. It was conventional Fifth Avenue, with the addition of a remarkable pipe organ. Many millionaires had a taste for organ music; when they built their dream houses, they liked to include the largest and finest organs they could afford—and these men could afford pretty much anything. Frank Woolworth's organ was piped all over the house, so that, for instance, organ music wafted out of bedposts. Woolworth had three daughters, and between 1911 and 1916 he had the architect C. P. H. Gilbert build three houses for them on the south side of East Eightieth Street. One of the daughters was the mother of Barbara Hutton, who spent much of her childhood at her grandfather's house. It was demolished in 1925, and the Stanhope Hotel, still standing, was built on the site. The three houses of the daughters still exist.

Also in 1899, when Franklin Woolworth began building, the Duke family, North Carolinians rich from the American Tobacco Company, began to penetrate Fifth Avenue. A mansarded house in the François I style with its long side on East Eighty-second Street was built in 1899 by a real-estate speculator and sold the following year to Benjamin Newton Duke. The house was known to the family as 2 East Eighty-second Street. Duke gave another house, 2 East Eighty-ninth Street, to his son when he married Cordelia Drexel Biddle.

Four blocks down Fifth Avenue was the grandest of the three Duke houses on Fifth Avenue. Twenty years earlier the speculator Henry Cook had purchased the entire block bounded by Fifth and Madison avenues and East Seventy-eighth and Seventy-ninth streets. He built his own house on the northeast corner of Seventy-eighth in 1883; for years, it was the only building on this extraordinary plot. The house was demolished in 1905, after his death, and the lot bought by James B. Duke, Benjamin Newton's brother. James B., known as Buck, was the most successful member of the Duke family. His jolly nickname belied a personality that was hot tempered, dictatorial, and somewhat grim. His nephew, Angier Biddle Duke, remembered, "Uncle Buck was a stern, somewhat distant figure, always dressed in a dark suit, high black shoes, a heavy gold watch chain, and a stiff white collar—even on fishing trips...." His house, always known as 1 East Seventy-eighth Street, was built in 1912 by Horace Trumbauer, a much-favored architect for the rich, who specialized in the palatial in much the same way as Richard Morris Hunt. His houses were less ornamented than Hunt's had been but even chillier. This was the house where Doris Duke, Buck Duke's only child, spent her lonely and overprotected (her father was terrified of kidnappers) childhood. In 1958, when there was only a handful of Fifth Avenue houses still in

The Dukes, multimillionaires from their American Tobacco Company, were one of the families whose multiple houses gave Fifth Avenue a series of family compounds early in the twentieth century. This photograph of the drawing room in the B. N. Duke house, taken in 1920, shows the fresh shift interior decoration made from the ponderous interiors of the late nineteenth century.

private hands, Doris Duke gave hers to New York University Institute of Fine Arts.

Horace Trumbauer's austere palace for Buck Duke was one of the final wave, lasting from about 1900 to about 1920, of single-family houses built on Fifth Avenue. There were not many of them, but they were very grand indeed.

When Payne Whitney, heir to the street railway fortune of his father, William C. Whitney, and to the Standard Oil fortune of his mother, Flora Whitney, married Helen Hay, daughter of John Hay, secretary and biographer of Abraham Lincoln, in 1902, his uncle Oliver Payne of Standard Oil gave him the plot on the old Cook property at 972 Fifth Avenue between Seventy-eighth and Seventy-ninth streets, just across a small garden from the Duke house, and commissioned Stanford White to design the house. The final cost, which included furniture, sculpture and works of art that White had selected in Europe, was said to be over one million dollars. Payne Whitney died in 1927, Helen Hay Whitney in 1944, and in 1952 the house became the French Embassy Cultural Services, a division of the French consulate.

Also in 1902, Andrew Carnegie completed his remarkable house on Fifth Avenue between East Ninetieth and Ninety-first streets. The house was sited so that it faced the northern side street and has always been known as 2 East Ninety-first. Carnegie bought the neighboring house at 9 East Ninetieth Street for his daughter Margaret Carnegie Miller and her son, Roswell Miller. The contractor for the house was David H. McAlpin, son of a family rich from tobacco and who were the builders of the McAlpin Hotel on West Thirty-fourth Street. It took a confident, self-made man like Carnegie to build in the neighborhood: both north and south exposures looked out on vacant lots; tenements and even shanties were not far away. The location possibly accounts for the heavy spiked fence that encloses the grounds. More than any other resident on Fifth Avenue, Andrew Carnegie created his own landscape. His house had about thirty thousand square feet of yard around it. By contrast, the Astor house at East Sixty-fifth Street had about one hundred square feet. It was built on the highest point of the Upper East Side of Manhattan and had extraordinary views down Fifth Avenue. The house, although no architectural gem, was so imposing that from 1903 on the area began to be referred to as Carnegie Hill. From the house Carnegie directed his extraordinary benefactions in the fields of libraries, music, and the peace movement. With an income of twenty-five million dollars a year, he gave away during his lifetime (he died in 1919 at the age of 84) about $350 million. Louise Carnegie, who survived her husband by twenty-seven years, lived in the house until 1946. From the 1940s to the 1960s the house was the Columbia University School of Social Work. In 1976 it became the Cooper-Hewitt, National Design Museum of the Smithsonian Institution.

When it was built in 1908, the Felix M. Warburg house on the northeast corner of Fifth Avenue and Ninety-second Street was the northernmost family mansion on Fifth Avenue except for the Jacob Ruppert house a

When Andrew Carnegie moved to New York from Pittsburgh, he bought the blockfront on the east side of Fifth Avenue between Ninetieth and Ninety-first streets on which to build his house, designed by Babb, Cook & Willard and completed in 1902. The Columbia University School of Social Work occupied the house from 1946 until 1976, when the Cooper-Hewitt Museum of Design moved in after extensive renovations by Hardy Holzman Pfeiffer Associates.

block away. The Warburg house was yet another in a French style, in this case Gothic, by C. P. H. Gilbert, with an open space to the north for a garden. The interiors echoed the outside and were rich in heavy furniture and tapestries. In 1944, Frieda Schiff Warburg gave the building to the Jewish Theological Seminary for its Jewish Museum, which opened in 1947. In 1962 a new entrance was built over the former lawn, and in 1993 that addition was torn down and a new wing erected in the same style, completing the Fifth Avenue front.

In 1914, William Starr Miller, described as a "retired capitalist," abandoned his huge house at 39 Fifth Avenue between East Tenth and Eleventh streets, next door to the Grosvenor Hotel, and built a new house on the very choice site on the southeast corner of Fifth Avenue and Eighty-sixth Street. Its style was generally described as Louis XIII; designed by Carrère & Hastings, it certainly was more restrained than the neighboring François I chateaux. Mrs. Cornelius Vanderbilt III (Grace Wilson) bought the Miller house after his death when she was finally obliged to give up her great house at 640 Fifth Avenue. Mrs. Vanderbilt,

Praised as one of the most distinguished buildings ever erected on Fifth Avenue, the William Starr Miller house on the southeast corner of Eighty-sixth Street was designed by Carrère and Hastings, architects of the New York Public Library, *and was completed in 1914. After Miller's death, the house was occupied from 1944 by Mrs. Cornelius Vanderbilt III until her death in 1953, and then by the YIVO Institute for Jewish Research.*

In 1914, Mr. and Mrs. Willard Straight commissioned the architectural firm of Delano & Aldrich to build a Federal-style town house rather unfashionably far up Fifth Avenue on the northeast corner of Ninety-fourth Street. Straight was a former member of the Chinese Imperial Customs Service and employee of J. P. Morgan, and married Dorothy Whitney, daughter of William C. Whitney. Together the Straights founded New Republic *magazine. The house is now the International Center of Photography.*

unchallenged as queen of New York society, regarded her removal as a great comedown—she referred to the Miller house as "the gardener's cottage"—but continued her industrial-scale entertaining there until her death in 1952.

Also in 1914 the firm of Delano & Aldrich built 1130 Fifth Avenue on the northeast corner of Ninety-fourth Street for Willard Straight. Its design was a far cry from a François I chateau, being a handsome and inviting American neo-Georgian. At the time it was built, this house was considered the "northernmost mansion on Fifth Avenue." The house later belonged to Mr. and Mrs. Harrison Williams. Williams appeared in New York City about 1908, selling automobile accessories; then he went into the rubber business. In neither of these businesses was he especially successful. He next went into public utilities and made a fortune. His wife, Mona, was famous for her clothes, her jewels, and her parties. She is generally considered the inventor of the "cult of black-and-white" in decor and clothes so characteristic of the art deco 1930s. The International Center for Photography opened in the house in 1974.

The last great private house built on Fifth Avenue and one of the grandest, was 1100 Fifth Avenue (always known as 1 East Ninety-first Street), across from Andrew Carnegie's house. It was built in 1918 for the banker Otto Kahn. Again, C. P. H. Gilbert was the architect, with J. Armstrong Stenhouse. Kahn was a German-Jewish financier who married into the banking firm of Kuhn Loeb. He was a notable patron of the arts, chairman of the Metropolitan Opera from 1908 to 1931, and donor of money to innumerable theatrical and dance companies as well as to individual writers like Hart Crane, who wrote his unforgettable New York poem *The Bridge* with a stipend from Kahn.

This enormous house spans six lots (145 feet on Fifth Avenue), with a total floor space of 13,000 square feet. Generally thought to be inspired by the Palazzo della Cancellaria in Rome and extremely Italian in feeling, the house, like the neo-Georgian Harrison Williams house, was a major departure from the French Fifth Avenue styles of the previous three decades. Because there were no more major mansions built on the avenue, however, the house has no descendants. René Gimpel, the Parisian art dealer, visited the house when it was complete. He said that although it was full of beautiful objects, Mrs. Kahn knew nothing of their history. "The art objects give as good as they get. They remained fixed there like street lamps that will never be lit."

Kahn died in 1934, and shortly after, the building was purchased by the Roman Catholic Convent of the Sacred Heart, which has used

Otto Kahn, notable financier and arts patron, built the last great private house on Fifth Avenue at Ninety-first Street in 1918. Designed by C. P. H. Gilbert with J. Armstrong Stenhouse, the 13,000-square-foot Italianate mansion signaled a departure from the French-style mansions of the previous three decades. After Kahn's death in 1934, the Roman Catholic Convent of the Sacred Heart purchased the house and has used it as a school.

it as a school. Among the generally brief tenures of most of the Fifth Avenue mansions by their original owners, this one is particularly striking, only sixteen years. The house suffered from being a latecomer; the age was already changing when it was built, and houses this size were becoming redundant.

By the time of World War I building on Fifth Avenue was solid to East Seventy-first Street, but north of that were vacant lots, seven between Seventy-first and Seventy-fifth streets and others farther north. "Millionaires' Row," stretching north up the avenue, did not consist only of huge new houses; some of the dwellings were still relatively modest and less lavish than some of those built on the side streets and Madison Avenue.

City assessments made in 1914 show just how valuable the prime residential real estate between East Sixtieth and Sixty-first streets was. The enormous house of the widowed Mrs. Elbridge T. Gerry on the southeast corner of Fifth Avenue and Sixty-first Street was assessed at $1.4 million. Its neighbor on the south, the Metropolitan Club, built

Temple Beth-el, at Fifth Avenue and the southeast corner of Seventy-sixth Street, was designed by William Arnold Brunner and Thomas Tryon, and dedicated in 1891. It was demolished in 1947 after the Reform Jewish congregation merged with Temple Emanu-el, built in 1929 at the northeast corner of Fifth Avenue and Sixty-fifth Street. Temple Beth-el featured among its architectural elements a Tiffany window, which was incorporated in the still-standing Temple Emanu-el.

Henry C. Phipps was one of the Pittsburgh millionaires, headed by Andrew Carnegie, who moved to New York around 1900. Phipps built his great Fifth Avenue house on the northeast corner of Eighty-seventh Street, just a few blocks below the mansion of his friend Carnegie. The neighborhood was a strange mix of vacant lots, shabby wooden houses, and glittering new mansions, and Phipps bought the lot across Eighty-seventh Street in 1905 for an astonishing $225,000 in an attempt to fend off undesirable neighbors. However, by the 1920s, the Phipps mansion was surrounded by new apartment buildings.

in 1894, was valued at cost, which was $2 million. Other valuations over $1 million included the John Jacob Astor house at East Sixty-fifth Street ($2,175,000); Thomas Fortune Ryan's house between Sixty-seventh and Sixty-eighth streets ($1,550,000); Henry Clay Frick's entire blockfront between Seventieth and Seventy-first streets, where the Lenox Library had stood ($3.1 million); William Andrews Clark's house on the northeast corner of Seventy-seventh Street ($4 million, the highest of all); and the James B. Duke house on the northeast corner of Seventy-eighth Street ($1,585,000).

The Real Estate Record and Guide pointed out the same year that the owners of most of the property had purchased it with the idea of building houses for their own use and were not speculating in land values. While that overstates the case, speculative building of townhouses was more characteristic of the side streets off Fifth Avenue. The magazine noted rather snobbily that upper Fifth Avenue "is one of the few sections of the city where rapid transit facilities are not essential, as all the residents have their private vehicles, which transport them to the nearest subway or

The Montana-made fortune of "Copper King" William Andrews Clark enabled him to make a splash in New York by building a "French Renaissance"–style house with 130 rooms, including twenty-one bathrooms and thirty servants' bedrooms, on the northeast corner of Fifth Avenue and Seventy-seventh Street. The architects, Lord, Hewlett & Hull, could hardly have been prepared for the criticism leveled at their work, which was brutally called an "eyesore," though such vituperation was probably aimed more at Clark, who was considered purse-proud and arrogant, than at the house itself.

When the Lenox Library was demolished, Henry Clay Frick, the Pittsburgh millionaire who controlled the largest coke and steel operation in the world, bought its site. There, architects Carrère & Hastings created a three-story marble palace in the Louis XVI style. The house was completed in 1914; Frick lived there only five years, until his death in 1919. John Russell Pope renovated the building between 1933 and 1935 for its current function as a museum.

elevated station." There were elevated lines on Second, Third, and Fourth avenues, and a street railway on Madison Avenue. (It is interesting to note that even millionaires were assumed to take public transportation.) Building proceeded quite irregularly: townhouses and eventually apartment houses and institutions, often with vacant lots interspersed.

The lifespan of Millionaires' Row was amazingly short; probably only in an American city could millions be spent on what was by the standards of Europe practically temporary housing. Although quite a few families owned several houses on Fifth Avenue—the Goulds, the Dukes, the Brokaws, and others—hardly a house was occupied by even two generations. Copper king William Andrews Clark's great hundred-room mansion, crammed on the too-narrow space on the northeast corner of Fifth Avenue at Seventy-seventh Street, was completed in 1911 and torn down in 1928, less than twenty years for a house generally conceded to be the most expensive town residence ever built in the United States. It was also one of the most disliked: architectural critics were outraged at its admittedly elaborate decoration; one compared it to the new jazz music "frozen in stone." There was even a smart-aleck verse about it in which Clark was supposedly the speaker:

> "I'll furnish a mansion, my latest whim
> That will render all squalid the home of him
> Who has dared to assert his claim to the throne
> Which I coppered long since as my special own."

Demolition of the private houses began about 1920 and accelerated in the following decade. (One critic said the best thing about the change was that the Clark house was torn down.) Owners sold mansions built by their fathers or even by themselves to developers, who put up apartment buildings or residential hotels. On the whole, the selling was not for a quick profit. Lack of money was seldom a cause for the tearing down of a mansion; the Whitneys, Dukes, and Phippses were not becoming poor, far from it. It was the life of private ballrooms, three-hour dinners, and footmen that was withering away. Suddenly, those things seemed a bother one could do without. A disdain for formality was emerging even before World War I. You had to live up to the standards of a fifty-room mansion on Fifth Avenue, and fewer of the rich wanted to exert themselves that way. Apartment living was equally luxurious but so much easier. As Simeon Strunsky, a commentator on New York life, wrote of Fifth Avenue in the 1920s: "…in the flush days of the bull market it was not primarily the cost of twenty servants that drove people into the apartment houses. It was the bother of housekeeping in a palace."

More entertaining was done in public places. The kind of people who lived in private houses on Fifth Avenue had once shunned publicity, or at

The Fifth Avenue Apartments opened in 1890 on the southeast corner of Fifth Avenue and Eighty-fifth Street. Multi-family buildings caught on slowly in New York, and the appearance of the Fifth Avenue Apartments was startling and unwelcome.

least professed to, and ladies in particular entertained little outside their own homes. Now, they got out and about and did not mind being seen in hotels, restaurants, and, increasingly, in nightclubs. There was much more weekending. Country homes were now close enough, thanks to the automobile and expanded transportation, for commuting into New York City; it is no coincidence that the end of private houses on Fifth Avenue

The twelve-story apartment building on the northeast corner of Fifth Avenue and Eighty-first Street was not the first apartment building on Upper Fifth Avenue, but it was the first luxury apartment building. The dignified Italianate building was designed by McKim, Mead & White, and was completed in 1912. Its vast apartments were clearly designed for rich tenants with large staffs. The building came under cooperative ownership in 1953.

in the 1920s coincided with the building of expensive homes on the North Shore of Long Island. More families settled for an apartment in town and a large suburban or country residence—and, of course, the family that gave up its house to move into one of the new apartments with eighteen rooms and eight maids' rooms was not giving up much in the way of luxury.

The WPA Guide to New York remarked in 1939, "Fifth Avenue, as well as other streets on the upper East Side, has been affected greatly by the postwar trend towards apartments. Its doom as Manhattan's last stronghold of single family homes seems certain." The great row of private houses stood vacant, many of them awaiting demolition. "The window shades are permanently drawn on Fifth Avenue and the doors and windows are often boarded up…," wrote Simeon Strunsky. "Now and then a glimmer of light betrays a hidden caretaker somewhere in the basement or a fifth story attic."

A few people on Upper Fifth Avenue already lived in apartments before the great demolition and building boom of the 1920s struck the avenue. A six-story apartment building at number 1038, known as the Fifth Avenue Apartments, was built in 1889–90 on the southeast corner of Eighty-fifth Street. It was rather modest, but met the same fate as its aristocratic townhouse neighbors, torn down in 1925 for the erection of a larger apartment house.

The forerunner of the great apartment buildings of the 1920s was 998 Fifth Avenue, the northeast corner of Eighty-first Street. It was not the first apartment house on Upper Fifth Avenue, but it was much the grandest in 1910, when it was built, and historically it is the most important: its efficiency and elegance helped make apartment living acceptable to the New York rich. The design by McKim, Mead & White was an immediate success, judged by favorable comment and an impressive list of tenants. In the future, it became clear, apartment houses would replace the private house. Upper-class New Yorkers had slowly been accustoming themselves to apartment living since 1869, when the Stuyvesant Apartments on East Eighteenth Street opened with a socially acceptable list of tenants that set it apart from mere tenements. By the turn of the century many well-to-do New Yorkers, families as well as bachelors, were accustomed to living, at least for short periods, at their clubs or in residential hotels; the transition to full-scale apartment living was not difficult, and 998 Fifth Avenue was constructed on so grand a scale that the apartments hardly differed from a private home.

Among the first tenants were Elihu Root, former U.S. secretary of state; Mrs. Elliott F. Shepard, granddaughter of Commodore Vanderbilt; and Murray Guggenheim, one of the seven Guggenheim brothers who created a great mining fortune. Root had been living in his own house, but Mrs. Shepard was already living in an apartment at the Buckingham Hotel on Fifth Avenue. For many years it was home to the richest woman in America, Sylvia Green Wilks, daughter of Hettie Green, the Witch of Wall Street, and widow of Matthew Astor Wilks. In 1926 she moved into a twenty-room duplex, including a penthouse, for which she paid $11,000 a year rent. In 1940 she exchanged it for two apartments on the third and fourth floors; she lived in the first and stored furniture in the second. When she died in 1951 at the age of eighty, she left an estate of $90,845,301, including $35 million in checking accounts that were drawing no interest. The estate was unique in that every cent was left to charity, sixty-three of them. At the time it was the largest estate ever bequeathed entirely to charity in the United States.

The architects of 998 Fifth Avenue constructed a series of townhouses stacked on each other. The twelve-story building had only two apartments per floor, each of fourteen or fifteen rooms and four bathrooms; some were duplexes. The dimensions were grand: in a typical apartment, a visitor arrived in a large elevator hall, then entered a large vestibule, which in turn led to the reception room, fourteen by thirty-six feet, from which one could enter either the salon, the living room, which measured twenty-one by twenty-four feet, or the dining room. Of the four master bedrooms, the largest measured seventeen by nineteen feet. There were six maids' rooms and a servants' hall. The renting agent was the young Douglas L. Elliman, beginning a career in the real-estate business that would last for decades. The building was rental (twenty-five thousand dollars per year was typical). It became a cooperative in 1953.

Number 998 was quickly followed by a series of apartment buildings, most of them about twelve stories tall and with only a few, but very spacious, apartments. In 1924, Michael Paterno, a prominent New York City builder, hired Warren & Wetmore, the architects of Grand Central Terminal, to design 1020 Fifth Avenue on the northeast corner of Eighty-third Street, replacing a townhouse. Rooms in the new building were, as the prospectus said, "of truly noble proportions"; the salons were twenty feet wide, forty feet long, and had ceilings eighteen feet high. The five-and-ten millionaire S. H. Kress bought a triplex apartment.

Number 845, at the southeast corner of Sixty-sixth Street (usually known as 4 East Sixty-sixth), was an eleven-story building in which a typical apartment, one to each floor, had eighteen rooms and six baths with seven servants' rooms and a servants' hall. At 820 Fifth Avenue on the southeast corner of Sixty-third Street, built in 1916, the entrance gallery was forty-three feet long, and each apartment had seven servants' rooms and a servants' hall. At 950 Fifth Avenue, on the northeast corner of Seventy-sixth Street, one of the apartments was a triplex with fifteen rooms and four baths. The reception room and dining room and four maids' rooms were on the first floor, four master bedrooms were on the second, and on the third, which was the roof, there was a solarium and card-room pent-house. On the other hand, number 825 had only two- or three-room suites with no kitchen and just a serving pantry to receive meals from a central restaurant. All these buildings still exist.

As more apartment houses were built on Fifth Avenue, their builders gained confidence and began innovations in design that went beyond stacking townhouses on top of each other. One of the earliest innovations was the penthouse, which immediately caught—and retains—the attention of the public and became synonymous with New York success. The idea of an apartment with a garden in the sky is irresistible. The top floors of buildings had formerly been the garrets, good enough for servants' rooms but otherwise useless. Nehered Agha of Condé Nast magazines, a close observer of the rich, said, "In Europe we live in garrets because we are poor, but in New York you can only live in the garret of a skyscraper if you are rich." Duplexes and triplexes—apartments occupying two and three floors, respectively—were also innovative and permitted architects more leeway in design.

For rental buildings leases were customarily calculated at two years for one- or two-room apartments, three years for four- to five-room apartments and five years for apartments of six rooms or more. The thinking behind this arrangement, unknown today, was that tenants with larger apartments would spend more on decoration but only if they had a longer lease.

Apartments in the buildings on Fifth Avenue between East Ninety-fifth Street and about East 102d Street that were put up in the great building era of the 1920s were noticeably smaller than those on lower blocks: eight or nine rooms with three baths were generally the largest. There was still a prejudice against building northward.

At number 1215, at the corner of 102d Street, was an apartment house built by the journalist Arthur Brisbane that incorporated his own apartment, bigger than most townhouses. Brisbane was the highest-paid newspaperman of his day, perhaps of any day in terms of purchasing power of money. In the early 1930s William Randolph Hearst paid him two hundred fifty thousand dollars a year to write a six-day-a-week column entitled "Today," which appeared on the front page of the Hearst tabloids and hundreds of other newspapers in the United States. Brisbane was astonishingly prolific: he wrote five hundred thousand words a year; in fifty-three years of journalism, he calculated that he had written twenty-five million words. Most of them might as well have been written on the wind so far as posterity was concerned. He was a master of superficiality and platitudes; his columns required the minimum effort on the part of readers; no long words, no opinions that would bewilder them. Although his superficiality was complete, he *was* energetic; he had a dictaphone (one of the earliest) in his car and crews of secretaries and messengers to rush his copy to the office of the *New York Journal,* his hometown outlet. His biographer wrote, "Few men, in this or any other age, have put on paper so seemingly endless an array of words, dealing with so seemingly endless a variety of topics. No man in the long history of journalism has been more widely and continuously read. No columnist ever enjoyed such a nationwide vogue, or was more unsuccessfully imitated."

He was also a skillful investor in New York City real estate; among other investments, he built the Ritz Tower, the forty-two-story apartment hotel at 109 East Fifty-seventh, on the northeast corner of Park Avenue, in

1925. When he died on Christmas Day of 1936, he left an estate of twenty-five to thirty million dollars.

Brisbane built 1215 Fifth Avenue in 1929 as an investment with a triplex apartment for himself on the fourteenth, fifteenth, and penthouse floors that could be reached by a private elevator from the street floor. The two-story living room measured twenty-six by sixty feet. There were nine bed-rooms. He was obviously inspired by the famous outsized apartment of his boss, William Randolph Hearst, whom he worshiped, at the Clarendon on West Eighty-sixth Street. A handsome bronze portrait medallion of Brisbane is set as a relief in the wall along the Fifth Avenue side of Central Park at 101st Street. A few doors north of Brisbane's palace Fiorello La Guardia lived at 1274 Fifth Avenue on the top floor of an unpretentious building.

Frederick Fillmore French, one of New York's most notable builders of the period (Tudor City, the Fred F. French Building on Fifth Avenue) also built an apartment house with a spacious and elaborate penthouse for himself and his family at 1010 Fifth Avenue on the northeast corner of Eighty-second Street. In 1923, French designed an unusual structure far north of the most fashionable district at East 109th Street and Fifth Avenue. The house, designed in the neoclassical style, was named Peace House. It was the creation of Mrs. J. Sargent Cram (Clare Bryce), member of a distinguished New York family that had long had a house on Washington Square. She was active in labor movements and in prison reform. She held antiwar meetings at Peace House for a few years; by the 1930s it was inactive. Mrs. Cram sold it in 1946; later it was occupied by charities. She was a woman of unusual ideas; she built, for example, an all-steel bungalow in Locust Valley, Long Island.

Even Arthur Brisbane's apartment or the S. H. Kress apartment seems insignificant when compared to cereal heiress Marjorie Merriweather Post's digs at 1107 Fifth Avenue, built in 1926. She put up the apartment building, rather than a townhouse, and reserved for herself an apartment of fifty-four rooms with a private driveway entrance on Ninety-second Street. The Post apartment on the twelfth, thirteenth, and penthouse floors included eighteen maids' rooms, "help's dining room," two "valet work rooms," a cedar closet, a "gown closet," a wine room, and a silver room with a safe. The decoration, judging from contemporary photographs, was an uneasy mixture of eighteenth-century French and English furniture, much of it reproduction, along with homey Americana. The general effect was hotel-like. Mrs. Post, as she called herself after her fourth divorce, spent very little time in this huge layout; the apartment was vacant for many years before it was converted into six nine-room apartments.

The idea of buying an apartment under a plan of cooperative ownership by the residents had been known in New York since the 1880s but had caught on slowly. By the time of the great Fifth Avenue building boom of the 1920s, however, the idea had become increasingly attractive to the kind of people who moved into the huge new apartments: under a cooperative plan a buyer could do as much with the space in his apartment as he could do in a freestanding house. Maintenance for cooperative apartments was generally calculated at an annual 10 percent of the selling price. As for typical prices, in 1931, 1040 Fifth Avenue offered cooperative apartments priced from $48,000 to $160,000.

The first tenants of the thirteen-story building at 960 Fifth Avenue, opened in 1929, then and now one of the grandest in New York, bought raw space and arranged the interiors of their apartments to fit their needs. The building contained duplexes and simplexes (one-floor apartments) arranged in very sophisticated ways. Dr. and Mrs. Preston Pope Satterwhite, for example, chose a duplex on the tenth and eleventh floors with seventeen rooms and nine baths, for which they reputedly paid $450,000. A curious arrangement in the huge apartment was the separation of the four maids' rooms from the three menservants' rooms by the entire width of the apartment, an architectural morality often found in large Victorian homes but seldom in New York apartments. There was a double internal staircase, not strictly necessary since the double height of the living room meant that the upper floor had space for only one master bedroom. Architectural historians have generally assumed that such staircases were intended for grand entrances of the hostess, but the steps were also used as tiered seats by guests "sitting out" at dances.

By no means all the private houses on Fifth Avenue were replaced by apartment buildings. When it became clear that single-owner housing on the avenue was doomed, institutions began buying, anxious for the prestige of a Fifth Avenue address and also anxious to buy cheaply property for which no one saw much future: in 1926, Marymount College bought number 1028, the Jonathan Thorne house on the southeast corner of Eighty-fourth Street; in 1946, Mrs. Edward King's house at number 991 between East Eightieth and Eighty-first streets became the American Irish Historical Society.

The Grand Army Plaza, divided in two by West Fifty-ninth Street at Fifth Avenue and the beginning of Millionaires' Row, was much improved, or at least changed, during the 1920s. Around 1900, the four sides of the plaza included the houses known as Marble Row and the great house of Cornelius Vanderbilt II on the south; the Savoy and Netherland hotels on the east; the Plaza Hotel on the west, all set against the backdrop of Central Park to the north. In 1903, Augustus Saint-Gaudens's dramatic equestrian statue of General William Tecumseh Sherman was dedicated on the north side, joined on the south in 1916 by a rather pale counterpart, the Pulitzer Fountain, donated by the newspaper publisher Joseph Pulitzer and surmounted, rather inexplicably, by the bronze figure of Pomona, goddess of abundance. The park entrance, the hotels, the private houses, the statuary, composed one of the finest urban landscapes in the world.

The exuberant late 1920s sought to improve even this grand setting: the Savoy and the Netherland hotels were torn down and a taller and more elegant Savoy-Plaza Hotel built in 1928, under the architects McKim, Mead & White. It had a forty-year existence, lasting until 1968, when the General Motors Company replaced it with 767 Fifth Avenue, designed by both Edward Durrell Stone and Emery Roth & Sons.

On the southeast corner of Sixty-first Street, replacing the grand house of Commodore (of the New York Yacht Club) Elbridge T. Gerry, was the Hotel Pierre, built by Schulze and Weaver in 1928. The name was taken from Charles Pierre, a great chef who had begun his career in the

catering business at Sherry's. The forty-four-story tower included seven hundred rooms. The daily rate was eight dollars for a single room. Most of the rooms were leased annually and after World War II became cooperative apartments. During the 1930s the Pierre was New York debutante headquarters. "Debs" lunched in its Georgian Room restaurant, where the table d'hôte was two dollars. Scotto, a pupil of Escoffier, was the chef. The original nightclub—all hotels had a nightclub in those days—was the Neptune Grill, decorated with pictures of fish and other deep-sea creatures under glass. The cover charge there was a hefty two dollars.

The Sherry-Netherland opened in 1927, designed, like the Savoy-Plaza, by Schulze and Weaver. There were 525 rooms in the forty-story edifice

Originally known as Jews' Hospital in the City of New York, Mount Sinai Hospital contructed ten buildings, all designed by Arnold W. Brunner, on Fifth Avenue at East 100th Street between 1898 and 1904. This 1929 photograph shows one of the old buildings being demolished to make room for a new wing. The hospital, now known as the Mount Sinai Medical Center, began expanding in the 1950s, employing the skills of many notable architecture firms, including Skidmore, Owings & Merrill, I. M. Pei, and Kahn & Jacobs.

on the northeast corner of Fifty-ninth Street and Fifth Avenue, most of them residential. The hotel, in fact, advertised itself as "more than a place to live—a new way of living."

North of Ninety-sixth Street, building on Fifth Avenue was sluggish, even during the great boom from the 1880s through the 1920s. Although the northern stretches of Central Park were among the greenest and quietest spots in New York, the avenue to the east attracted only a relatively few townhouses and apartment buildings. The impetus to build came, instead, from institutions, particularly hospitals, which occupied ever-increasing amounts of the best building lots.

Beginning in 1904, Mount Sinai Hospital was built between East Ninety-eighth and 102d streets and the Fifth Avenue Hospital (later called Flower and Fifth Avenue Hospitals and now Cardinal Cook Health Care Center) between East 105th and 106th streets in 1921. The Heckscher Foundation for Children, which also housed the New York Society for the Prevention of Cruelty to Children, occupied a building between East 104th and 105th streets (now El Museo del Barrio). The neighborhood became an important center for medical research when the New York Academy of Medicine constructed a distinctive building, massively Lombardian Romanesque, at the southeast corner of 103d Street in 1926.

Even the statuary in the neighborhood had medical themes: the statue of Dr. J. Marion Sims on Fifth Avenue opposite 103d Street commemorates a medical pioneer, a gynecologist who in 1855 founded Woman's Hospital of the State of New York. He was a Southerner who during the Civil War moved to Europe but returned to become president of the American Medical Association.

7

Above
the Park

110th Street to 145th Street

•

Attempts have been made off and on to refer to West 110th Street from Fifth Avenue to Central Park West as *Central Park North,* but the term has never fallen easily from the tongues of New Yorkers. The fourth side of the park has always lacked the cachet of the other three. New apartment houses lined the street early in this century, never so elegant as those along Fifth Avenue, but dignified, middle-class in appearance. When Harlem's population became largely black in the early 1920s, the street was known as the "golden edge" of Harlem; living there was a sign of achievement.

Above 110th Street the constant northward development of Fifth Avenue ran for the first time into an already developed community. Although there were some residents in Harlem from the Dutch era of New York onward, they never numbered more than a few thousand. The expansion and prosperity of Harlem in the late nineteenth century really was due to improved transportation: elevated trains reached Harlem in the 1880s. The two decades that followed were a golden age for an increased population, largely Jewish and immigrant, many of them moving up, in every sense of the word, from the Lower East Side. They lived in brownstones, smaller than those lower on Fifth Avenue but solid in comfort. In 1917 there were eighty thousand Jews in Harlem. They were not there for long: by 1930 there were only about five thousand, the neighborhood having become largely resettled by blacks emigrating from the South and the Caribbean. Fifth Avenue was the western border of East Harlem, also largely Jewish until its population became Italian and Spanish and divided itself into "Italian Harlem" and "Spanish Harlem" in well-defined neighborhoods. A few blocks of Fifth Avenue between 110th and 116th streets were part of Spanish Harlem in the 1930s, when there were Spanish-speaking merchants and two movie houses, the Teatro Latino and the Teatro Hispano, both of which showed Spanish-language films.

Along Fifth Avenue around 1900 there were enclaves of well-to-do white Protestants, easy to locate by their large and handsome churches, Episcopal, Presbyterian, and Baptist mainly, a number of which survive. The Protestant settlement centered around Mount Morris. This little park, sitting astride Fifth Avenue between 120th and 124th streets, takes its name from the Morris family, colonial gentry and landowners whose name is also preserved in Morrisania in the Bronx, and from an outcropping of rock in its middle, which has always been too large to level.

Mount Morris was the perennial victim of municipal indifference. Lack of interest on the part of city government is shown by the timetable of Mount Morris's history: in 1836 Mount Morris Square was named; in 1861 plans were made for the square to be graded and turned into a municipal park; nothing had been done by 1874, when there was an engineers' report strongly criticizing the municipal government for its inactivity; in 1887 the city finally got around to planting grass and trees, and putting a fence around the plot, and there finally was a Mount Morris Park.

The elevation of Mount Morris, at a time when height was valued, made it a prime location for firewatching. New York City was the victim of constant destructive fires: major conflagrations in 1835, 1839, and 1845 destroyed hundreds of buildings, entire blocks, in just the one decade. There was an inadequate supply of water, the firefighters were mainly volunteers and not entirely reliable, and most buildings were made of wood.

Mount Morris Park, originally Mount Morris Square, was a rocky outcropping that interrupted Fifth Avenue between 120th and 124th streets. Because of its elevation, the square was the site of the fire watchtower pictured here, from which an employee of the city surveyed for smoke and flames. Long unsettled because of its inhospitable terrain, the area was discovered by upper-middle-class settlers in the later half of the nineteenth century, and, as better transportation availed itself, became a desirable place to live.

Before the telephone, there was no quick way of spreading a fire alarm. So the city relied on fire towers with a man on round-the-clock duty to ring a bell when he spotted the outbreak of a fire from his perch. A cast-iron fire watchtower, the only one surviving in Manhattan, was erected in Mount Morris Park in 1856.

Around Mount Morris Park, handsome residences were built in the 1890s, both single-family houses and apartment buildings. The neighborhood was regarded as a coming one for well-to-do families. They were great church builders: those still standing include the Mount Morris Baptist Church at 2050 Fifth on the west side of the avenue between 126th and 127th streets (built 1888) and the Episcopal Church of St. Andrew at 2067 Fifth on the northeast corner of 127th Street (1891).

Mount Morris declined with the rest of Harlem in the second half of the twentieth century. The park itself was renamed Marcus Garvey Memorial Park, and at the same time a recreation center and swimming pool were added. Garvey was a Jamaican who settled in Harlem in 1917 and founded the United Negro Improvement Association, a black pride

Mount Morris Park was noted for its churches, including the First Baptist Church of Harlem, on the west side of Fifth Avenue between 126th and 127th streets, which was destroyed by fire in 1873. It was replaced by a stone church, which is still standing and is now known as Mt. Moriah Baptist Church. The houses on either side of the church are typical of the freestanding, single-family houses first built in the neighborhood. By 1900, fewer and fewer of these remained as large apartment buildings began to surround Mount Morris Park.

organization that in the 1920s became a back-to-Africa movement, buying ships (the Black Star Line) to transport black American settlers to Liberia. The movement collapsed with charges of mismanagement and fraud. Garvey was convicted of mail fraud, imprisoned, served his term, and deported back to Jamaica.

Just above the two churches on West 127th Street at 2078 Fifth Avenue, on the northwest corner of 128th Street, lived the most famous Fifth Avenue hermits—probably the most famous hermits in American

In the 1890s, cycling became a major recreational activity, due largely to the invention of the pneumatic tire and the paving of streets that had been uninvitingly cobblestoned. The sport was considered groundbreaking because women as well as men participated. Cycling clubs were formed and shops supplied new cycling fashions and accesories. Upper Fifth Avenue was an extremely popular place to ride, as this 1896 photograph looking south from East 115th Street shows. The signboard surrounding the tree, at right, advertises products for riders.

history—the Collyer brothers. In comparison with them, Fifth Avenue's other recluses, the Wendel family, appear positively sociable.

Early in the twentieth century one of the families occupying a brownstone in the highly respectable neighborhood consisted of Dr. and Mrs. Collyer and their two sons, Langley and Homer Collyer. The family were well educated and had cultivated tastes. Homer graduated from Columbia College in 1904, Langley was an accomplished pianist. From what little is known of the Collyers' background, however, it is clear there was something amiss in the family's life. The doctor and his wife separated, and the two sons stayed with the mother, who seems to have dominated them. Homer worked for a few years as a title researcher; Langley, it seems, never worked at all. Mrs. Collyer died in 1929, and her sons became increasingly reclusive, living on rents from various parcels of real estate in the city. Services to 2078 Fifth Avenue, such as electricity, were cut off because bills were ignored by the Collyers.

In 1938, Helen Worden (later Erskine; her husband was John Erskine, a Columbia professor who wrote the successful novel *The Private Life of Helen of Troy*), then a reporter for the *New York World* talented at sniffing out strange New York stories, discovered that Langley and Homer had barricaded themselves in their house behind piles of bricks and mounds of newspapers. After long silent-hour watches on the street, she found Langley, who occasionally came out at night to shop for peanut butter, which the Collyers mainly lived on, and cornered him for a brief chat. He said, "We purposely make our home look as if no one lived in it....We've no telephone. And we've stopped opening our mail. You can't imagine how free we feel."

In 1942 the brothers were about to be evicted from the house because for years they had ignored their mortgage payments. The house was invaded by lawyers, the sheriff, city marshals, and a locksmith, while crowds, including Helen Worden, watched. Reluctantly emerging, Langley finally paid the mortgage in cash and withdrew into his citadel.

On 21 March 1947, on an anonymous report of Homer's death, police entered the house or, rather, attempted to. The entire house was booby-trapped, so that any intruder risked being crushed by bricks and stones. The body of Homer, who was blind, was found after fifty tons of trash had been hauled out by city workmen. He had starved to death. After nineteen days of dredging, Langley's body was found. The victim of one of his own booby traps, he had been buried under an avalanche of bricks.

The story of the Collyers fascinated New York and the country. Crowds gathered daily in front of the house while workmen, justifiably apprehensive of more booby traps, cautiously removed the contents. There were, of course, rumors that great treasures would be found, but there was little of value; even fourteen pianos were beyond repair, not to speak of the chassis of an automobile found in the basement.

The steady decline of Harlem after World War II did not spare Fifth Avenue, which saw its one-family brownstones degenerate into rooming houses and its better shops close. Almost the only building above 110th Street has been for public housing. On the east side of the avenue between 138th and 142d streets, the Riverbend Houses, 625 rent-subsidized apartments, were opened in 1967. The architects were Davis, Brody and Associates. At one of the bleakest corners of Fifth Avenue, East 110th Street, where there was nothing but filling stations, Arthur A. Schomburg Plaza was built in 1975 as a project of the New York State Urban Development Corporation. Arthur Schomburg was a Puerto Rican of mixed black-white parentage who amassed a famous collection on black history that he sold in 1926 to the New York Public Library; the collection became the nucleus of the Schomberg Center for Research in Black Culture. The two thirty-five-story octagonal buildings on Fifth Avenue named for him were designed by Gruzen & Partners and, like the Riverbend Houses, have been much praised for their design.

Epilogue

•

The physical presence of Fifth Avenue was little affected during the prosperous years after World War II ended; not many new buildings, commercial or residential, joined those constructed during the boom of the 1920s. With the 1960s came another wave of construction, to continue, with occasional dull periods during recessions, for thirty years. New construction, mostly office buildings with shops on the street floor, centered in the busy blocks between Thirty-fourth and Sixtieth streets, where there was some of the heaviest pedestrian traffic in the world. That section of Fifth Avenue remained the most fashionable shopping street in America. Further downtown, between Fourteenth and Thirty-fourth streets there was a continuing decline into loft buildings and cheaper shops. Between Fourteenth and Washington Square was a stable, largely residential neighborhood with little new construction except number Two Fifth Avenue, a huge white apartment house on the northwest corner of Washington Square, opened in 1950 over the loud objections of neighborhood preservationists. The great landmarks—the Empire State Building, the New York Public Library, Rockefeller

Center, the Metropolitan Museum of Art—continued to dominate Fifth Avenue. Nothing so grand was added to the streetscape.

Only a few new apartment buildings joined the majestic line along Central Park from Sixty-first to Ninety-sixth streets. Those that did seemed fragile in comparison to the stately edifices of the 1920s and, although expensive, were anything but patrician in appearance. The new buildings failed to meet with universal approbation. Number 1001 Fifth Avenue, for example, between Eighty-first and Eighty-second streets, designed by Philip Johnson, a tall limestone building with a make-believe (and easily detectable) mansard roof, was judged bluntly by the AIA *Guide to New York City* to be "an architectural conceit raised to new heights." The neo-Georgian town house of Mrs. Marcellus Hartley Dodge (Geraldine Rockefeller), at 800 Fifth Avenue, was replaced in 1978 by a tall apartment building fronting Fifth Avenue with a three-story false wall, necessary to meet zoning requirements, but visually quite unconvincing.

Changes in the ownership of buildings, of which there were many following World War II, had little effect on the physical appearance of the avenue. The private house as residence was extinct; the townhouses that survived were transformed into the headquarters of institutions—foundations, cultural societies, schools, charities, or foreign consultates and missions. The Archer M. Huntington house at 1083 Fifth Avenue between Eighty-ninth and Nintieth streets, a late (1914) mansion designed by Ogden Codman, became the home of the National Academy of Design and its art school in 1958, and the same year, the James B. Duke house on the northeast corner of Fifth Avenue and Seventy-eighth Street became the New York University Institute of Fine Arts. The choice of upper Fifth Avenue by the institutions was due more to the lure of large space at the best address than any special desire to preserve notable architecture, and from the preservationist point of view the results were decidedly mixed. Private houses, even the grandest, were not really suitable for institutional purposes: the grand rooms were too large and the servants' and service rooms too small. Partitions had to be erected, parquet covered with institutional carpeting, and fine interiors ruthlessly pulled about to make office space; there was seldom enough money for proper adaptation to new purposes. Facades remained at least, and the elegant scale of the neighborhood was largely retained.

The major new museum construction on Fifth Avenue in the post-war years was the Solomon R. Guggenheim Museum, striding the block between Eighty-eighth and Eighty-ninth streets. The patron whose name it carried was a member of a German-Jewish family who made a fortune in mining. The Guggenheims had a long association with Fifth Avenue; by 1900, several members of the family had town houses on the avenue, and Solomon himself, who was noted for his style and extravagance, lived in the Plaza Hotel in an endless suite. He had a wife, as well as numerous less permanent arrangements.

Guggenheim was only somewhat interested in art collecting when, in the 1920s, he met a Prussian woman who called herself Baroness Hilla Rebay von Ehrenwiesen. Overweight, loud, argumentative, and bossy, she somehow cast a spell over Solomon Guggenheim, who spent a great deal of money on her and her enthusiasms. She was addicted to movie fan magazines and to chocolates, painted abstract pictures, and was a fanatic advocate for non-objective art (Wassily Kandinsky and Paul Klee were artists she particularly admired) about which she wrote weighty books in obfuscatory German-American. Under her guidance, Guggenheim, who never did anything by halves, bought scores of paintings by her favorite artists, including a large number of acknowledged masterpieces of twentieth-century art.

The next step was to open a museum so the public could be impressed with the new art: in 1937, Rebay became the curator of Guggenheim's collection and in 1939, the Museum of Non-Objective Painting opened on Fifty-fourth Street, exhibiting mainly works by Kandinsky and Klee. As early as 1943, Guggenheim determined to build a major museum for his collection, to stand in the most conspicuous place in New York, that place being, of course, Fifth Avenue. He bought the blockfront between Eighty-eighth and Eighty-ninth streets and demolished half a dozen town houses standing there. He commissioned Frank Lloyd Wright, who had never been asked to design any important building in New York and notoriously hated the city, perhaps for that reason, to draw up plans for a museum. The building was still on the drawing board when Guggenheim died in 1949.

In the early 1950s, the plans were submitted to city officials. They were not notably enthusiastic, and it was seven years before building permits were finally issued. The museum opened on 21 October 1959, a strange event with none of the principals present: the patron was dead (his family carried out his wishes), the architect had died six months earlier; Hilla von Rebay was at odds with the Guggenheim heirs and forbidden the premises; and the first director, James Johnson Sweeney, had just left after a dispute with the trustees.

The Guggenheim building was immediately identified as a monument to the architect rather than a showcase for art. Its swirling shape called forth all sorts of hilarious comparisons: a snail and a melting ice-cream cone were the most popular. The best of many cartoons showed a bewildered passerby asking another, "Are they allowed to do that on Fifth Avenue?" Two additions, both somewhat controversial, have since been erected.

Farther down the avenue at the Plaza, where Central Park begins, one of the most obvious, not to say startling, changes on Fifth Avenue in decades came during the building boom of the 1960s. The Savoy-Plaza Hotel, between Fifty-eighth and Fifty-ninth streets, and its surrounding shops, an integral part of the noble streetscape around Grand Army Plaza, fell to the wreckers. For the site, the General Motors Corporation commissioned a white skyscraper from architects Edward Durrell Stone and Emery Roth & Sons. The new building opened in 1968. The street floor above a sunken plaza was used as a showroom in which new model automobiles revolved on platforms under massive chandeliers. The incongruity of selling automobiles in one of the world's great pedestrian areas did not escape critics, nor did the loss of varied street-level shops and restaurants. The chilliness was somewhat relieved in 1986, when

F. A. O. Schwarz, New York's most famous toy store, established in the city since 1870, moved into the downtown street floor of 767 Fifth Avenue, as the General Motors building is officially known, and crowds of eager youngsters did something to restore the pedestrian life for which the plaza was designed.

In 1976, Olympic Tower, a skyscraper building, opened at 641 Fifth Avenue, the northeast corner of East Fifty-first Street across the street from St. Patrick's Cathedral, a prime and historic location where the Roman Catholic Boys' Orphan Asylum had once stood, followed in 1900 by the Union Club, then the Grand Central Galleries, an art dealership, from 1932 on. Olympic Tower, designed by Skidmore, Owings & Merrill, was "mixed use," layered with shops on the street floor, above them offices, and apartments on the top. Duplexes, one with a swimming pool, occupied the top two floors.

Another mixed-used building, taller and even grander, followed: Trump Tower at 725 Fifth Avenue, the northeast corner of Fifty-sixth Street, opened in 1983. Designed by the architect Der Scutt, the dazzling glass building wrapped itself around Tiffany's on the Fifty-seventh Street side, and the East Fifty-sixth Street facade was stepped with shimmering glass boxes on which trumpeters performed carols at Christmas. Condominium apartments with extraordinary views, a shopping arcade with thirty-five retail stores, a waterfall, and marble everywhere made it the most sumptuous building ever to open on Fifth Avenue.

Olympic and Trump Towers restored residential living, at least for a well-heeled few, on a section of Fifth Avenue that had not been residential for half a century. Farther north, the district beginning at East Sixty-first Street remained "millionaires' row." The row began, as it had for more than a century, at number 795 Fifth Avenue (the Pierre Hotel) and continued thirty-five blocks to number 1148 at Ninety-sixth Street. In the early 1990s, these thirty-five blocks contained fifty-one buildings that were cooperative apartment houses, three condominium apartment buildings, and two family-owned townhouses, the other buildings being institutional.

Although for more than a century the row's advantage has supposedly been its views of Central Park and the better light and air from the park, in truth, for renters and purchasers the Fifth Avenue address has always been the main attraction. Only about half the apartments on Fifth Avenue face the park. The best buildings, many now seventy-five years old, are collectively termed "pre-war," meaning built before World War II; several are actually pre-World War I. Those apartments command prices so premium it is clear Fifth Avenue has lost none of its appeal for the rich.

The term "pre-war" implies solid and conservative structures, dignity, and apartments with the spaciousness and specialized rooms (servants' dining hall, silver safe) of the earliest buildings, although, in fact, by mid-century few of them preserved their original graciousness. Many apartments had been reduced in size during the Depression or World War II, but a seventeen-room apartment cut in half still produced two apartments that seemed luxurious.

With occasional setbacks, the Fifth Avenue real estate market remained strong, and prices, for the most part, advanced relentlessly. It was news when a Fifth Avenue pre-war cooperative apartment sold for a million dollars in the 1970s; then there were reports of a five million dollar apartment in the 1980s; and in the 1990s several, all in pre-war buildings, sold for ten million dollars or more.

Changes made by new owners in the layouts and amenities of these enviable apartments were frequently drastic: many were "gutted" (considered a positive, even flattering, word by owners and the architectural press) and entirely rebuilt. New buyers rivalled each other in the extent—and expense—of their changes. Ripping out architectural features, even those installed by a recent predecessor, came to be regarded as a measure of good taste. Walls were no longer sacred, nor were ceilings and even windows. Insofar as generalizations are possible, the trend was to reduce the number of rooms, four bedrooms becoming two, for example, in response to smaller families and the contemporary desire for a spacious look. Servants' rooms were joined to make one large bedroom or storage space (one owner had an entire room built for her shoes), or eliminated altogether. The cost of these large-scale changes often equaled the purchase price of the apartment.

While the decor of the apartments was more eclectic than it had been in the nineteenth century, there was still a "Fifth Avenue look," or, rather, a series of looks changing from time to time. In the 1950s, for example, Fifth Avenue taste was often described as a French eighteenth-century marble-topped commode with an African mask sitting on it and a small Renoir nude hanging over it. Later, a sort of English country house look prevailed in the unlikely setting of noisy New York, with bright chintz, needlepoint cushions, small dog portraits, and alabaster obelisks on the mantels. There was an echo of nineteenth-century Fifth Avenue only in the curtains, still over-valanced, over-pleated, and puffy.

Below the residential neighborhood, retailing maintained its pre-eminence for many blocks downtown. Patches of decay appeared at intervals; the Fifth Avenue Association ceaselessly battled to maintain the elegance of the avenue by closing tacky stores "going out of business" (announced by large, hand-written signs) for years and street peddlers who threatened to turn the avenue into an outdoor bazaar.

At the end of the twentieth century Fifth Avenue ranks first in most surveys of the world's most expensive retail space, the second most expensive area being the intersecting East Fifty-seventh Street. International design and entertainment enterprises, Versace, Piaget, Takashimaya, and the Walt Disney store have taken the places of firms like Best & Co., Bonwit Teller, and Gorham Silver. None put up new buildings, instead making over storefronts and interiors at enormous cost. Number One East Fifty-seventh Street, the northeast corner of Fifth Avenue, where Mary Mason Jones's Marble Row had once stood in lonely splendor surrounded by vacant lots and grazing goats, for example, had been occupied since 1930 by a much-admired art deco office building by Cross & Cross. In 1993, the building became the home of Warner Brothers, not the corporate headquarters as it might have been in the 1960s, but the company's retail shop.

Naturally, there were outcries against the newcomers, reminiscent of the commotion one hundred-fifty years earlier when the first shops appeared on the avenue, and claims that their generally flamboyant presence cheapened the avenue. To most New Yorkers, however, the new establishments demonstrate once again the endless ability of Fifth Avenue, like New York City, to renew and reinvent itself. And no wonder new businesses want to locate on Fifth Avenue: pedestrian traffic was estimated in the late 1990s at fifty million people a year. In 1923, Robert C. Holliday, an essayist, called Fifth Avenue "that glamorous national possession of ours, the most gorgeous and imposing show street in the land." Seventy-five years later its glamour has changed but glows as bright as ever.

Along Fifth Avenue, a decade before its second century begins, are ranged an extraordinary mix of retail businesses, institutions, and residences. Some of the finest shops in the world and some of America's noblest public buildings line the avenue, but Fifth Avenue is also the home address of more than twenty-five thousand people, some living in ten million dollar penthouses, others in subsidized housing. Still the long chalk line down the island of Manhattan, the all-important dividing line between the East Side and the West Side of the island is an international symbol of fashion and wealth. At the same time, it is essential New York in its startling contrasts, beginning with a marble arch in an old patrician square and ending six and a half miles north in abandoned buildings and used car lots. But the glamour is stronger than ever, a stroll on the Avenue is as tonic as ever it had been, and, for millions, Fifth Avenue is the finest street and the best address in the world.

Bibliography

•

The Fifth Avenue Bank, an aristocratic institution legendary for the consideration it lavished on well-to-do clients and very conscious of its history, published *Fifth Avenue: Glances at the Vicissitudes and Romance of a World-Renowned Thoroughfare…* (New York: The Fifth Avenue Bank, 1915), a well-written seventy-six-page booklet by an anonymous writer; on the hundredth anniversary of Fifth Avenue, it commissioned the historian and antiquarian Henry Collins Brown to write the still-useful *Fifth Avenue Old and New, 1824–1924* (New York: The Fifth Avenue Bank, 1924).

Louise Frances Reynolds, writing anonymously, produced a short (nineteen pages) work on Fifth Avenue entitled *The History of a Great Thoroughfare* (New York: Thoroughfare Publishing Co., 1916).

Arthur B. Maurice's *Fifth Avenue* (New York: Dodd, Mead & Co., 1918) is an impressionistic work, mainly captions for the plates, but with some insights into the history of the avenue.

The Fifth Avenue Association on its half-century anniversary published *Fifty Years on Fifth, 1907–1957* (New York: The Fifth Avenue Association, 1957). Theodore James, Jr.'s *Fifth Avenue* (New York: Walker, 1971) is a lively survey illustrated with vintage photographs and photographs commissioned for the book. Kate Simon's *Fifth Avenue: A Very Social History* (New York: Harcourt Brace Jovanovich, 1978) is marred by deplorable errors and absurd misinterpretations. Ronda Wist's *On Fifth Avenue Then and Now* (New York: Birch Lane Press, 1992) is a good history of retail stores and shopping on the avenue.

Always at hand while I was writing this book were the six volumes of I. N. Phelps Stokes's magisterial *The Iconography of Manhattan Island, 1498–1909* (New York: Robert H. Dodd, 1915–1928) and John A. Kouwenhoven's *The Columbia Historical Portrait of New York City* (New York: Harper and Row, 1953). Other books useful for the history of Fifth Avenue are:

Alpern, Andrew. *Historic Manhattan Apartment Houses.* New York: Dover Publications, 1996.

The Architecture of McKim, Mead & White. New York: Dover Publications, 1990.

Armstrong, Hamilton Fish. *Those Days.* New York: Harper & Row, 1963.

Armstrong, Maitland. *Day Before Yesterday: Reminiscences of a Varied Life.* New York: Charles Scribner's Sons, 1920.

Baker, Paul R. *Richard Morris Hunt.* Cambridge, Mass.: MIT Press, 1980.

Baker, Paul R. *Stanny: The Gilded Life of Stanford White.* New York: Free Press, 1989.

Beard, Rick, and Leslie Cohen Berlowitz. *Greenwich Village: Culture and Counterculture.* New Brunswick: Rutgers University Press, 1993.

Botkin, B. A. *New York City Folklore.* New York: Random House, 1956.

Boyer, M. Christine. *Manhattan Manners: Architecture and Style, 1850–1900.* New York: Rizzoli International Publications, 1985.

Brevoort, Henry. *The Letters of Henry Brevoort to Washington Irving.* New York: G. P. Putnam's Sons, 1918.

Britt, George. *Forty Years—Forty Millions: The Career of Frank A. Munsey.* New York: Farrar and Rinehart, 1935.

Brown, Eve. *The Plaza: Its Life and Times.* New York: Meredith Press, 1967.

Brown, Henry Collins. *Brownstone Fronts and Saratoga Trunks.* New York: E. P. Dutton & Co., 1935.

Brown, Henry Collins. *In the Golden Nineties.* Hastings-on-Hudson: Valentine's Manual, 1928.

Brown, Henry Collins. *Valentine's Manual of Old New York, Vol. 2.* New York: Valentine's Manual, 1917–1918.

Butler, William Allen. *A Retrospect of Forty Years, 1825–1865.* New York: Charles Scribner's Sons, 1911.

Callender, James. *Yesterdays in Little Old New York.* New York: Dorland Press, 1929.

Carlson, Oliver. *The Man Who Made the News: James Gordon Bennett.* New York: Duell, Sloan and Pearce, 1942.

Carlson, Oliver. *Brisbane: A Candid Biography.* New York: Stacpole Sons, 1937.

Churchill, Allen. *They Never Came Back.* New York: Doubleday, 1960.

Crockett, Albert Stevens. *Peacocks on Parade: A Narrative of a Unique Period in American Social History and Its Most Colorful Figures.* New York: Sears Publishing Co., 1931.

Cromley, Elizabeth C. *Alone Together: A History of New York's Early Apartments.* Ithaca: Cornell University Press, 1990.

Crowninshield, Frank, ed. *The Unofficial Palace of New York: A Tribute to the Waldorf-Astoria.* New York: The Waldorf-Astoria, 1939.

Dain, Phyllis. *The New York Public Library: A History of its Founding and Early Years.* New York: The New York Public Library, 1972.

Dau's New York Blue Book. New York: Dau Publishing Co., 1914–37.

Dunn, William J. *Knickerbocker Centennial: An Informal History of the Knickerbocker Club, 1871–1971.* New York: The Knickerbocker Club, 1971.

Edmiston, Susan, and Linda D. Cirino. *Literary New York: A History and Guide.* Boston: Houghton Mifflin, 1976.

Erskine, Helen Worden. *Out of This World.* New York: G. P. Putnam's Sons, 1953.

Federal Writers' Project. *The WPA Guide to New York.* New York: Pantheon, 1982.

Floyd-Jones, Thomas. *Backward Glances: Reminiscences of an Old New-Yorker.* New York: 1914.

Gray, Christopher, ed. *Fifth Avenue, 1911: From Start to Finish in Historic Block-by-block Photographs.* New York: Dover Publications, 1994.

Gurlock, Jeffrey S. *When Harlem Was Jewish, 1870–1930.* New York: Columbia University Press, 1979.

Harrison, Constance Cary. *The Anglomaniacs.* New York: Cassell Publishing Co., 1890.

Harrison, Constance Cary. *Recollections Grave and Gay.* New York: Charles Scribner's Sons, 1911.

Helmstreet, Charles. *Nooks and Corners of Old New York.* New York: Charles Scribner's Sons, 1899.

Henderson, Helen W. *A Loiterer in New York.* New York: George H. Doran, 1917.

Holliday, Robert Cortes. *In the Neighborhood of Murray Hill.* New York: George H. Doran Co., 1923.

Hoyt, Edwin P. *The Goulds: A Social History.* New York: Weybright and Talley, 1964.

Josephy, Helen, and Mary Margaret McBride. *New York is Everybody's Town.* New York: G. P. Putnam's Sons, 1931.

King, Moses. *King's Handbook of New York City.* Boston: 1893.

Lewis, Arnold; James Turner; and Steven McQuillin. *The Opulent Interiors of the Gilded Age: All 203 Photographs from "Artistic Houses."* New York: Dover Publications, 1987.

Lewis, Arthur H. *The Day They Shook the Plum Tree.* New York: Harcourt, Brace & World, 1963.

Lockwood, Charles. *Manhattan Moves Uptown.* New York: Barnes and Noble, 1995.

McCabe, James D., Jr. *New York by Gaslight.* New York: Greenwich House, 1984.

McCarthy, James Remington. *Peacock Alley: The Romance of the Waldorf-Astoria.* New York: Harper & Brothers, 1931.

McCullough, Esther Morgan, ed. *As I Pass, O Manhattan.* New York: Coley Taylor, 1956.

Mack, Edward C. *Peter Cooper, Citizen of New York.* New York: Duell, Sloan and Pearce, 1949.

Matthews, Brander. *These Many Years: Recollections of a New Yorker.* New York: Charles Scribner's Sons, 1917.

Mayer, Grace M. *Once Upon a City: New York from 1890 to 1910 as Photographed by Byron.* New York: Macmillan, 1958.

Morris, Lloyd. *Incredible New York.* New York: Random House, 1951.

Nevins, Allan. *The Evening Post: A Century of Journalism.* New York: Russell & Russell, 1968.

New York City Landmarks Preservation Commission. *Metropolitan Museum Historic District Designation Report.* New York: 1977.

O'Connor, Richard. *The Scandalous Mr. Bennett.* Garden City: Doubleday & Co., 1962.

Parry, Albert. *Garrets and Pretenders: A History of Bohemianism in America.* New York: Covici-Friede, 1933.

Reed, Henry Hope. *The New York Public Library: Its Architecture and Decoration.* New York: W. W. Norton, 1986.

Ross, Ishbel. *Crusades and Crinolines: The Life and Times of Ellen Curtis Demorest and William Jennings Demorest.* New York: Harper & Row, 1963.

A Picture of New York in 1846 with a Short Account of Places in its Vicinity . . . . New York: C. S. Francis & Co., 1846.

Powell, Dawn. *Diaries, 1931–1965.* South Royalton, Vt.: Steerforth Press, 1995.

Saltus, Edgar. *Vanity Square: A Story of Fifth Avenue Life.* Philadelphia: J. B. Lippincott, 1906.

Saucier, Ted. *Bottoms Up.* New York: Greystone Press, 1951.

Shackleton, Robert. *The Book of New York.* Philadelphia: Penn Publishing Co., 1920.

Stern, Robert A. M.; Gregory Gilmartin; and John Montague Massengale. *New York 1900: Metropolitan Architecture and Urbanism, 1890–1915.* New York: Rizzoli International Publications, 1983.

Stern, Robert A. M.; Gregory Gilmartin; and Thomas Mellins. *New York 1930: Architecture and Urbanism Between the Two World Wars.* New York: Rizzoli International Publications, 1987.

Stewart, William Rhinelander. *Grace Church and Old New York.* New York: E. P. Dutton, 1924.

Still, Bayard. *Mirror for Gotham: New York as Seen by Contemporaries from Dutch Days to the Present.* New York: New York University Press, 1956.

Stokes, I. N. Phelps. *New York Past and Present . . . Compiled . . . on the Occasion of the New York's World Fair.* New York: Plantin Press, 1939.

Strunsky, Simeon. *No Mean City.* New York: E. P. Dutton & Co., 1944.

Sullivan, Mark. *Our Times: The United States 1900–1925.* New York: Charles Scribner's Sons, 1926.

Thomas, Lately. *Sam Ward, "King of the Lobby."* Boston: Houghton Mifflin, 1965.

Towne, Charles Hanson. *This New York of Mine.* New York: Cosmopolitan Book Corp., 1931.

Townsend, Reginald T. *God Packed My Picnic Basket.* New York: The New England Society in the City of New York, 1970.

Townsend, Reginald T. *Mother of Clubs: Being the History of the First Hundred Years of the Union Club of the City of New York, 1836–1936.* New York: 1936.

Van Every, Edward. *Sins of New York as Exposed by the Police Gazette.* New York: Frederick A. Stokes, 1930.

Wall, E. Berry. *Neither Pest nor Puritan: The Memoirs.* New York: The Dial Press, 1940.

Weitenkampf, Frank. *Manhattan Kaleidoscope.* New York: Charles Scribner's Sons, 1947.

Willensky, Elliot, and Norval White. *AIA Guide to New York City.* 3d ed. New York: Harcourt Brace Jovanovich, 1988.

Wilson, Rufus R., and Otilie E. *New York in Literature.* Elmira: Primavera Press, Inc., 1947.

Wright, Mabel Osgood. *My New York.* New York: The Macmillan Company, 1926.

Index

•